THE TOTAL ACOUSTIC GUITARIST

A Fun and Comprehensive Overview of Acoustic Guitar Playing

FRANK NATTER, JR.

Alfred, the leader in educational publishing,

and the National Guitar Workshop,

one of America's finest guitar schools, have joined

forces to bring you the best, most progressive

educational tools possible. We hope you will enjoy

this book and encourage you to look for

other fine products from Alfred and the

National Guitar Workshop.

Alfred Publishing Co., Inc.
16320 Roscoe Blvd., Suite 100
P.O. Box 10003
Van Nuys, CA 91410-0003
alfred.com

Copyright © MMVI by Alfred Publishing Co., Inc.
All rights reserved. Printed in USA.

ISBN-10: 0-7390-3851-6 (Book & CD)
ISBN-13: 978-0-7390-3851-2 (Book & CD)

*This book was acquired, edited and produced
by Workshop Arts, Inc., the publishing arm of
the National Guitar Workshop.
Nathaniel Gunod, acquisitions, managing editor
Burgess Speed, editor
Matthew Liston, assistant editor
Timothy Phelps, interior design
Ante Gelo, music typesetter
CD recorded by Mark Schane-Lydon at WorkshopLive.com, Pittsfield, MA*

*Cover guitar courtesy of Taylor Guitars.
Cover photograph: © iStockphoto.com / Jordan Chesbrough*

Table of Contents

About the Author

Frank Natter, Jr. is a guitarist, composer and teacher. He has performed in folk, rock, blues and contemporary ensembles across the United States. In collaboration with guitarist Frank L. Natter, Sr. and modern dance choreographer Linalynn Schmelzer, Frank, Jr. has composed original music for dance. He has also been commissioned by visual artist Roslyn Brault to create music for video. These works were premiered at Yale University, Greater Hartford Academy, A. P. E. Theater in Northampton, MA and the University of Massachusetts at Amherst. Frank studies composition and arranging with accomplished musicians such as Charles Sutton, Brian K. Kershner and Charles P. Menoche. Currently, Frank brings his diverse acoustic guitar techniques to the acoustic duo Facets. Facet's debut CD, *Facets,* was recorded in 1998 and was followed by *Over the Blue Land,* recorded live in 1999 and released in 2000.

Frank is involved in youth music programs, teaches adult guitar classes and gives private instruction at his studio—Face Arts Music—located in Deep River, Connecticut.

PHOTO BY TIMOTHY RYAN PHELPS

Acknowledgements

Thank you to Burgess Speed for his insight and the opportunity to put these ideas down on paper; to Madlyn Bynum for her encouragement; to my family for their support; to all my teachers for their guidance; and to my students for the inspiration they give.

0
Track
0.0

A compact disc is available with this book. Using the disc will help make learning more enjoyable and the information more meaningful. Listening to the CD will help you correctly interpret the rhythms and feel of each example. The symbol at the upper left appears next to each song or example that is performed on the CD. Example numbers are above the symbol. The track number below each symbol corresponds directly to the song or example you want to hear. In most cases, there is more than one example per track; this is reflected in the track numbers (for example: track 2.1, track 2.2, track 2.3, etc.). Track 1 will help you tune to this CD.

Introduction

Welcome to *The Total Acoustic Guitarist,* a beginning-to-advanced acoustic guitar method designed to provide students with a strong foundation of acoustic guitar techniques and styles. As you explore the pages of this book you will uncover ways to strum chords, pick patterns, play solos and construct songs. You'll find that acoustic techniques are rooted in the rich traditions of folk, bluegrass and blues, yet the fusion of these traditional styles has led to many new contemporary and rock-driven tricks-of-the-trade.

How to Use This Book

The book is divided into two sections:

- **Part 1: Playing Acoustic Songs** gets you acquainted with your instrument and reading standard music notation, TAB and the diagrams in this book. Also, you'll strum chords to songs and learn how chords are built. Finally, you'll put down the pick and try your hand at fingerstyle.

- **Part 2: Acoustic Styles** teaches you the techniques behind foundational acoustic guitar genres such as bluegrass and blues. You'll discover how modern rock guitarists use the acoustic guitar to vary the textures of their music. You'll be able to recognize and name the parts of a song and examine songwriting techniques used by guitarist-songwriters. Finally, you'll look at some progressive ways to play the guitar in new tunings and with new left- and right-hand techniques. You'll even take a quick look at some world music influences on the acoustic guitar.

To get the most out of this book, you should go through Part 1 first. Don't get hung up on any one lesson. If something seems to be giving you difficulty, move on and come back to it. Later chapters will prompt you to refer to important information introduced in earlier chapters. After getting an overall understanding of Part 1, move on to Part 2.

Each chapter of Part 2 is a self-contained set of lessons. Once you have the skills acquired in Part 1, you can go through the chapters in Part 2 in any order that interests you.

Enjoy yourself as you use this book to build a versatile technique that allows you to incorporate many genres into your own unique approach to the acoustic guitar. Have fun!

PART 1: Playing Acoustic Songs

Chapter 1: Getting to Know the Acoustic Guitar

Lesson 1: Parts and Positioning of the Guitar

This chapter covers general acoustic guitar and musical concepts. You may find it helpful to refer to this chapter if you have any questions about holding the guitar, naming notes on the neck, tuning, reading chord diagrams and scale diagrams, interpreting tablature and standard music notation. Feel free to either browse this chapter for specific answers to your questions or to read it in its entirety.

Parts of the Acoustic Guitar

Acoustic Guitar

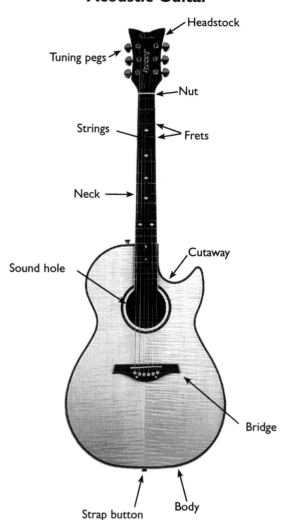

- Headstock
- Tuning pegs
- Nut
- Strings
- Frets
- Neck
- Cutaway
- Sound hole
- Bridge
- Strap button
- Body

Holding the Guitar

There are three typical ways to hold the acoustic guitar:

1. You may choose to sit in the *folk position* with your guitar resting on your right leg.

Folk position.

2. You may prefer the *classical position* and rest your guitar on your left leg, which is usually raised by a footstool.

Classical position.

3. You may find that wearing a strap and standing is most comfortable.

   The method that works best for you is the one that keeps your guitar stationary even if your left hand is not touching the neck. You must be relaxed and your left hand must be free to press the strings against the fretboard at various locations.

Home Base for the Left Hand

You should develop a "home-base" positioning for your left hand, which you may stray from only for musical reasons. At home base, the small joint of your thumb should be unbent, behind the neck, and aligned with your 2nd finger. Your four fingers should curve over the neck, with their small joints directly above the string or strings you mean to push against the fretboard. To form "fretted" tones, you set the very tips of your fingers slightly to the left of the frets and press for as long as you want the tones to ring. Never push more than is necessary to produce clear sounds. For purpose of communication, the left hand fingers are numbered from 1 to 4 starting with the index finger. The picture to the right shows the numbering of the fingers.

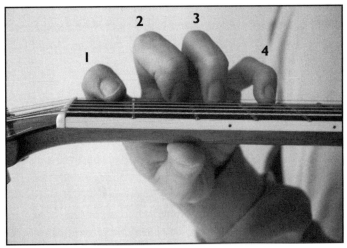

Finger numbers and correct position of left hand.

The Right Hand

Your right hand is used to strike the strings, either with a pick or with the fingers. To strike the strings with a pick, you hold it between your thumb and index finger, pointing the tip of the pick toward the strings (see picture to the right). With a twist of the forearm, you move the pick across the strings in a downward or upward motion. When the pick moves downward, toward the floor, you should angle its tip slightly upward. Likewise, when the pick moves upward, you should angle its tip slightly downward. Again, the key is staying relaxed. There's no need to squeeze the pick extra hard. Don't worry if you occasionally drop it. This will occur less and less as you become comfortable with the slight angling of the pick. Many acoustic songs are played using right-hand fingers to strike the strings. This technique is called *fingerstyle* and has a few variations that we'll discuss in detail in Chapter 6 (see page 48).

Correct right-hand position.

Lesson 2: Naming Pitches

The Musical Alphabet

We use the first seven letters of the alphabet to name *pitches* (musical sounds of a particular highness or lowness of tone). These letters, A–B–C–D–E–F–G, are the *musical alphabet* or *natural notes*. To name all the pitches we can play, we must repeat the musical alphabet. In other words, the note that is one letter name higher than G is called A and will sound similar but noticeably higher than the original A. The next pitch after that is a higher version of B, then a higher C, and so on. Likewise, the note that is one letter name lower than A is the note G (see right).

The Natural Notes

A–B–C–D–E–F–G, A–B–C–D–E–F–G, A–B–C–D–E–F–G, etc.

The Musical Alphabet

Half Steps and Whole Steps

The smallest distance between two pitches is one fret. This distance is called a *half step*. A two-fret distance is a *whole step*. Only two pairs of natural notes are a half step apart. These are B–C and E–F. All the rest of the natural notes are a whole step apart, including G–A where the musical alphabet repeats.

Sharps and Flats

There are no frets between the half steps B–C and E–F. But there is a fret between other neighboring notes of the musical alphabet. The fret between two natural notes is named after either of the natural notes beside it, and its letter name is modified by a *sharp* or *flat* symbol.

♯ This is the *sharp* symbol. It tells you to play the pitch one half step *higher* than the natural note it modifies.

♭ This is the *flat* symbol. It tells you to play the pitch a half step *lower* than the natural note it modifies.

♮ This is the *natural* symbol. It cancels any previous sharps or flats and tells you to return to the natural version of the note.

Enharmonic Equivalents

Here are two ways to name all the possible notes between A and A:

A – A♯ – B – C – C♯ – D – D♯ – E – F – F♯ – G – G♯ – A

A – B♭ – B – C – D♭ – D – E♭ – E – F – G♭ – G – A♭ – A

The notes in gray are *enharmonic equivalents*. These are pitches that sound exactly the same but have different letter names.

The String Names

Guitar strings are referred to by number or letter name. The 1st string is the thinnest and the 6th string is the thickest. A string is named after the "open" pitch that it sounds when no left-hand fingers are pressing it. To be able to name all the notes on the fretboard, it is necessary to commit the names of the strings to memory.

Pitch Name	Low E	A	D	G	B	High E
String Number	6	5	4	3	2	1

All the Notes on the Fretboard

To name any note on the neck, all that you need to remember is the names of the strings and the fact that only the notes B–C and E–F do not have a sharp or flat between them. Below are all the notes on the guitar neck from the open strings to the 12th fret.

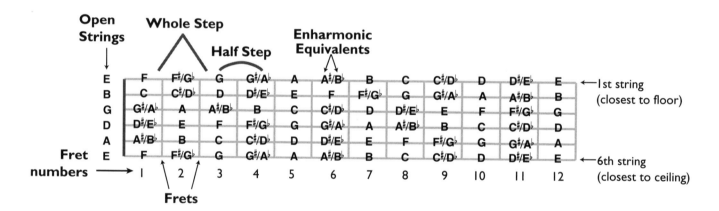

Lesson 3: Tuning

Being able to keep your guitar in tune is necessary for making good music. There are a few different ways you can tune.

The Electronic Tuner

Perhaps the best way to begin tuning is with the help of an *electronic tuner*. You can pick one up at any local music store. Electronic tuners are easy to use. You just need to be familiar with the string names (the diagram below should help with that). The idea is to get in tune in any way that works for you so your ears can get used to the sound of strings that are correctly tuned.

Matching Open Notes

Track 1 of the CD for this book sounds six pitches—E, A, D, G, B and E—that correspond to the open strings of your guitar. You can match your open strings with these pitches. This will assure that you will be in tune with the examples on the CD. Otherwise, you can match your strings to the same notes on a piano, as shown in the diagram at the bottom of the page.

Relative Tuning

If you don't have access to an electronic tuner, the CD or a piano, you might have to tune your strings by relating the sound of one string to the sound of another; this is *relative tuning*. If it's been a while since you've tuned your guitar, make sure that your 6th string doesn't seem extra tight or extra loose before proceeding with this method.

Follow these steps, using the diagram below as a guide:

1. Play the A note at the 5th fret on the 6th string.

2. Compare it with the open 5th string, which should be the same A note as the fretted 6th string.

3. If the open 5th string doesn't match the fretted 6th string then adjust the 5th string until it does.

4. Carry this procedure to the next sets of strings using the diagram below as a guide.

5. Notice that the fretted B note on the 3rd string is at the 4th fret when all the rest of the tuning notes are found on the 5th fret.

Relative Tuning Diagram

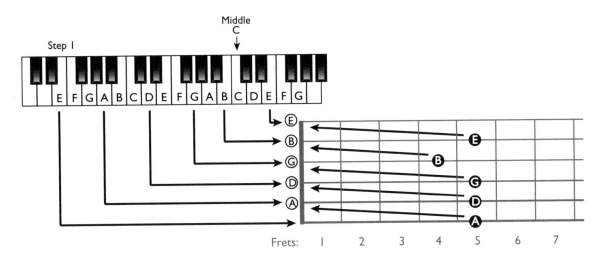

Lesson 4: Music Notation

This book uses standard music notation, tablature, chord diagrams and scale diagrams to communicate musical examples.

Standard Music Notation

Another way to represent the musical alphabet is by using the five-line, four-space musical *staff*. Each line and space of the staff represents a letter of the musical alphabet. When a note **o** is placed on a line or a space, it tells a musician to play the pitch that the line or space represents. Guitar music is written in the *treble clef* 𝄞 (also known as G clef). This clef encircles the 2nd line from the bottom and tells us that this line represents the note G. From that reference note we can continue the musical alphabet above and below the G line (see below).

Musical Alphabet on the Staff

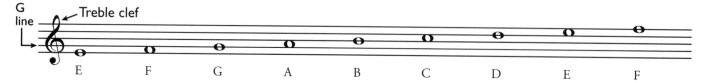

Some musicians find it helpful to memorize the notes on the spaces and the notes on the lines separately. Coincidentally, two devices can be used to help. The space notes spell the word "FACE," and the line notes can be memorized using the first letter of each word in the saying: "**E**very **G**ood **B**eginner **D**oes **F**ine."

Space notes   **Line notes**

Ledger Lines

As we mentioned in Lesson 2 (page 7), the musical alphabet repeats itself to accommodate the pitches we play from lowest to highest. The lowest notes that we can play are actually *too low* to fit on the staff, just as the highest notes that we can play are *too high* to fit on the staff. To solve this problem we use *ledger lines*, which are temporary extensions to the staff. They are used only with notes that don't fit on the staff. Here's what notes lower than E (the **E** of **E**very) and notes higher than F (the **F** of **F**ine) look like when written in standard music notation.

Notes Above and Below the Staff

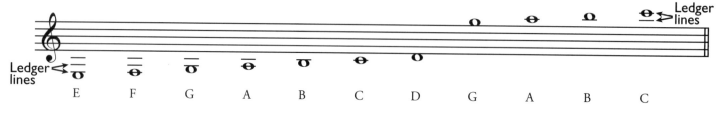

Tablature

Tablature, or TAB, is a system used only for guitar and other fretted instruments. There are six lines that represent the strings (not notes). Numbers are placed on the lines; these numbers tell you what frets to play. Numbers under the TAB staff tell you which left-hand fingers to use. The top line represents the 1st string and the bottom line represents the 6th string. In this book, TAB is written below the corresponding standard music notation.

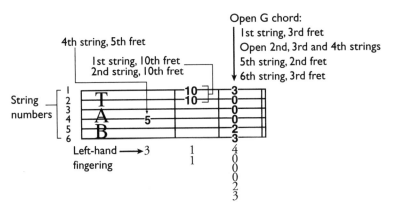

Chord Diagrams

A *chord* is three or more notes played at the same time. A *chord diagram,* which is oriented vertically, illustrates the fretboard and shows you the position, shape and fingering for a chord. To decipher a chord diagram, imagine that you are facing your guitar while it is resting on a guitar stand.

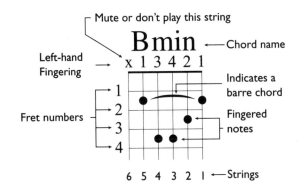

Scale Diagrams

Scale diagrams use similar indications as chord diagrams except that they are horizontal representations of the guitar neck as opposed to the vertical layout of the chord diagram. They can be used to illustrate different concepts but are most commonly used to display scale fingerings.

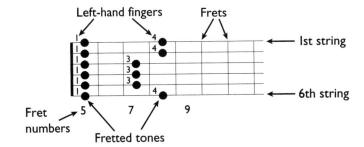

Chapter 2: Warming Up

Now it's time to get moving around on the guitar. After playing through this chapter you'll be using all four left-hand fingers, strumming rhythms and changing chords in time. Take as much time as you need here, as these skills will be helpful later. Also, you can use the accompanying CD and the examples in this chapter to guide your daily warm-ups as you progress through the rest of this book and learn songs.

Lesson 1: The Four-Finger Stretch

Here's a warm-up that will quickly bring your left-hand fingers to home-base position (see page 7). Only the TAB is given, because we have not talked about another important aspect of standard music notation, rhythm (see page 13).

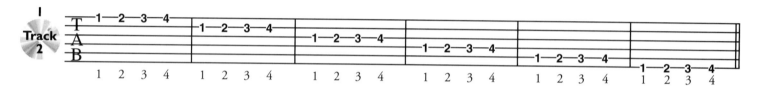

To get the most out of this stretching exercise, try to remind yourself of these guidelines:

1. As you place a finger down on a string, don't lift the ones placed before it. Leave all fingers down until you cross to a new string; then release and start fresh on the next string.

2. Don't push harder to get a note to sound. Try to move your finger closer to the fret instead. Breathe and stay relaxed.

3. Spend no more than five minutes on this exercise each time you play; do your best to remember these guidelines; and try again another day.

If this stretch feels particularly hard, try playing the entire exercise in the 5th *position* (see below) and working your way back down to the 1st position over the course of weeks.

> **Position**
>
> A *position* is the four-fret span that your left-hand fingers can reach naturally when your 1st finger lines up to a fret and the others stretch out. Positions are named for the fret to which your 1st finger is designated.

Four-Finger Stretch at the 5th Position

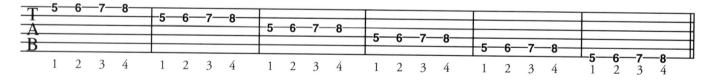

Lesson 2: Counting Rhythm

Rhythm is the combination of long and short sounds and silences and is an essential element of music.

The Beat

The *beat* is an even, constant pulse. When we clap or tap to a song we are aligning our movement with the beat.

The Measure

Songs make us feel beats in groups called *measures*. The most common grouping is the four-beat measure. As you read the staff from left to right, you'll see vertical lines called *bar lines*; these mark the locations on the staff where one measure ends and the next begins.

The Time Signature

The actual number of beats-per-measure is designated by the *time signature,* two numbers (one over the other) at the beginning of the music next to the clef (see Chapter 1, Lesson 4, page 10, for the definition of clef). The four-beat measure is labeled by the time signature symbol $\frac{4}{4}$.

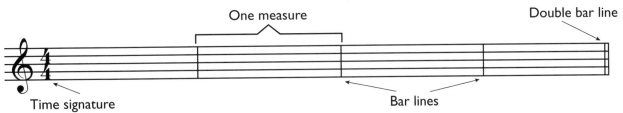

One measure   Double bar line

Time signature   Bar lines

Note Values

In Chapter 1 (page 10), we talked about notes and their letter names. Now, let's complete our understanding of standard note symbols by changing their appearance based on their *note value* or duration. The value and appearance of a note is determined by the number of beats for which it sounds (see chart below).

Note Values

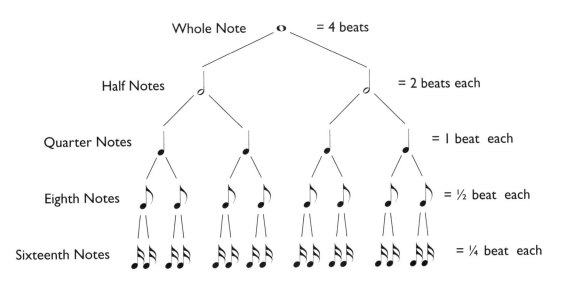

Whole Note = 4 beats

Half Notes = 2 beats each

Quarter Notes = 1 beat each

Eighth Notes = ½ beat each

Sixteenth Notes = ¼ beat each

Often, we divide a beat into two parts. The first part, the *onbeat,* occurs at the moment our foot hits the floor (as we tap along to the beat). The second part, the *offbeat,* occurs as our foot is in the air (between onbeats). Eighth notes ring for less than a beat. In fact, two consecutive eighth notes fill one beat. The first eighth note sounds on the onbeat and second one sounds on the offbeat.

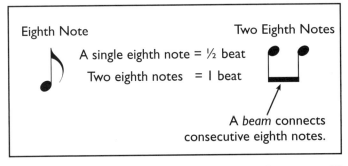

Eighth Note — A single eighth note = ½ beat
Two eighth notes = 1 beat

Two Eighth Notes — A *beam* connects consecutive eighth notes.

Count a steady beat aloud as you play this example of whole notes, half notes and quarter notes. This example uses only the open 1st string. Try playing along with the CD until you get the count.

Now, try adding some eighth notes. The eighth notes on the onbeats should be played with *downstrokes* ⊓ of the pick and the eighth notes on the offbeat should be played with *upstrokes* ∨ of the pick. Count the onbeats with beat numbers and the offbeats with "&" (pronounced "and").

⊓ = Downstroke
∨ = Upstroke

Rests

Interesting rhythms often incorporate silences. Silences in music are indicated by *rests*. There is a rest symbol that corresponds to each note value. Think of silence as something you must play (as you play pitches) and count rests the same way you count notes.

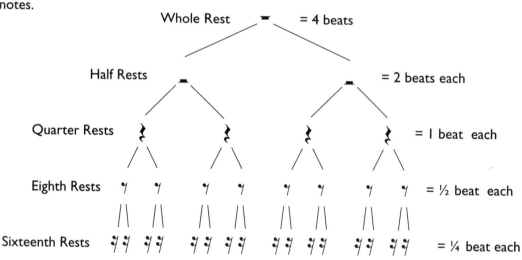

Try this rhythm incorporating rests. To play these rests, rest your pick on the 1st string to stop its sound; or stop the string from ringing with your left hand. Notice the counting numbers for rests are in parentheses.

This *repeat sign* tells you to repeat once from the beginning.

Lesson 3: Strumming

When providing rhythm to a song, guitarists often move the pick across three or more strings at once to create one big sound. This motion is called *strumming* and the big sound, made up of three or more notes, is called a *chord*.

The Amin Chord

Try placing your fingers on the fretboard to form the five-string A Minor (Amin) chord to the right. Once you're lined up, give it a strum by moving your pick downward across the 5th through 1st strings in one quick motion. Twist your forearm (as if you were turning a door knob), and then spring it back to ready position above the 5th or 6th string. You can get rid of any muted or buzzing notes by remembering to press the strings on the very tips of your fingers so that each finger only touches the string it's fretting. For the cleanest tone, your fingers should be as close to the frets as you can manage. (It's alright if your 2nd finger needs to slide back a little to make room for your 3rd.)

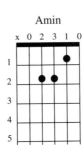

Amin

The Down-Up Motion

Most strummed rhythms combine downstrokes and upstrokes. When strumming, your pick should move in a constant alternating down-up motion sometimes hitting the strings and sometimes passing over them. Strums that fall on downstrokes tend to be fuller in sound because the pick moves across all the strings of the chord. Strums that fall on upstrokes will be lighter, as the pick gently attacks just two or three strings. If you let this occur naturally in your strumming, your rhythms will have a strong musical flow.

Rhythmic Notation

Strumming passages often use *rhythmic notation*. This system indicates rhythm, but no pitch, using slightly altered note symbols (see below). Chords symbols appearing above the rhythm tell us what chords to play and on which count to change them. Guitar music is written in TAB, standard music notation and rhythmic notation. Sometimes all three are used within a single song.

Rhythmic Notation Values

Try the rhythm below, paying close attention to your picking motion.

Lesson 4: Changing Chords

Let's learn a few new chords and how to change between them as we keep a steady count and the constant down-up pick motion. First, here's a C chord.

The C Chord

Compare the fingering of the C chord to that of the Amin chord. Notice that the 1st and 2nd fingers are on the same frets.

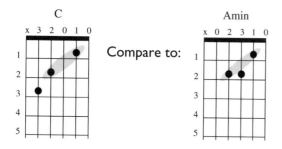

Feeling Consistent Fingers

The key to smooth chord changes is minimal motion and recognizing consistent fingers. When learning new chord changes try to search for similarities between chords. Focus on these consistencies, as it will make challenging changes seem easy.

Let's focus on the similarities between the Amin and C chords following these steps:

- **Step 1:** Finger the diagonal shape that is in both chords.
- **Step 2:** Now finger an Amin chord.
- **Step 3:** Return to the consistent shape.
- **Step 4:** Finger a C chord without lifting off the consistent diagonal shape.
- **Step 5:** Repeat this a few times, trying to make the change without allowing any tension in your 1st and 2nd fingers.

Now try some strumming rhythms using both chords. The first rhythm uses half notes and quarter notes. The chords change on beat 1 of the measure. It will help to move your pick in time to the beat even when there isn't a strum on the beat.

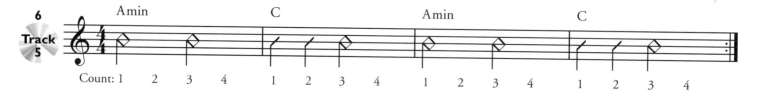

Now add some eighth notes. Remember to keep a constant down-up pick motion with light upstrokes.

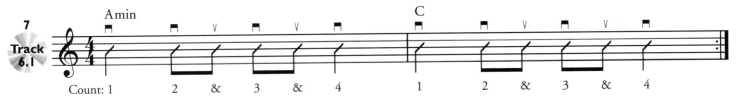

The D Chord

Comparing the D chord to the C chord, you can see that there aren't any consistent fingers between the two chords. So, to change between these two chords we must have a different method of attack.

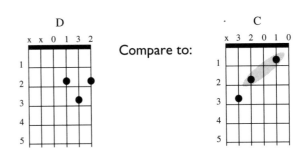

Compare to:

Forming Chords in Midair

Often, there will not be much in common between two chord fingerings, as is the case of the C and D chords. The trick here is to become so familiar with the two chords, that you can *form them in midair* as you lift your fingers to make the change.

Try this exercise to learn how to form the D chord in midair.

1. Form the chord. Take as much time as you need to place your left hand comfortably.

2. Release the pressure from the strings, while still feeling them under your fingertips.

3. Keeping the shape of the chord, lift your fingers about an eighth of an inch from the strings.

4. Then press your fingers down on the chord again and strum.

5. Totally relax, then repeat these steps a few times.

You can use this process to give your fingers a "memory" of any new chord shape. Once you can easily form the D chord, try this process for the C chord. If you can form both chords in midair then you will easily be able to change between the two in a song. When you're comfortable with the two chords, try the rhythm below (example 8).

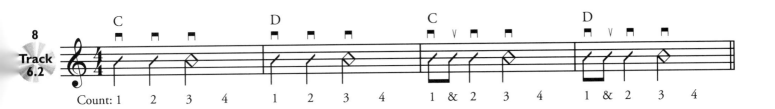

Now, try this one that combines chords with consistent fingers (Amin and C) and chords that you have to form in midair because they do *not* have consistent fingers (C and D).

Root Notes and the Bass-Strum Technique

All chords have a principal note. This *root* note gives the chord its letter name. In *root position,* it is the bass note of the chord, the lowest note you strum. For example, the lowest note in the Amin chord is "A" played on the open A string; so, A is the root note. Often, guitarists separate the root from the rest of the chord when strumming rhythms. They first attack the bass and then strum the rest of the chord. This *bass-strum technique* produces the sound of two parts happening at once.

Here's an example of this bass-strum technique written in tablature with chord symbols above.

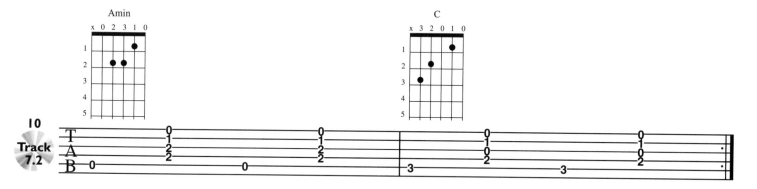

More on Chord Names

A chord name has two parts, a letter name (A, C, etc.) and a chord *quality,* or type (major, minor, etc.). The letter name on the left of the symbol tells us the root of the chord. The chord type—to the right of the letter name—tells us if the chord is minor or something more colorful. A chord symbol with a letter name alone is understood to be a major chord (for example, "C" is a C Major chord), while a chord name such as "Amin" tells us that the chord is a minor type chord with an A root. Chord construction will be discussed in detail in Chapter 4 and Chapter 5 (pages 33 and 39).

Slash Chords

You'll sometimes run into chord names such as D/A or C/G. These are *slash chords* and are used when a song calls for a note other than a chord's root note in the bass. The symbol on the left side of the slash is the actual chord, while the letter on the right side of the slash is the chord's temporary new bass note. Below are two examples of slash chords. We will make use of slash chords throughout this book, as they give the bass some independence and make music interesting.

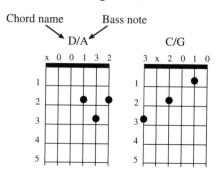

Chapter 3: Songs in G, D and C

This chapter will get you playing chords to songs in three *keys*. A key is a specific set of seven notes (we'll talk about this in detail in Chapter 4, page 29). Each note of a key can be used as the root note for one of seven different chords from that key. Of the seven chords in a key, three are used most frequently in songs. In this chapter we'll focus on these three chords called the *primary chords* as well as some minor chords common to each key.

Lesson 1: The Primary Chords in G

Here are the three primary chords in the key of G Major.

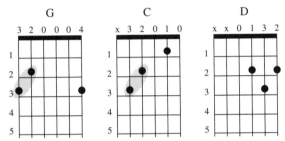

Consistent fingering shape is in gray.

Let's practice changing these chords with a progression of the primary chords in the style of Van Morrison's "Brown Eyed Girl." To learn this tune quickly, focus on the consistent diagonal shape of your 2nd and 3rd fingers between the G and the C. Also, practice changing from G to D using the midair technique (see page 17).

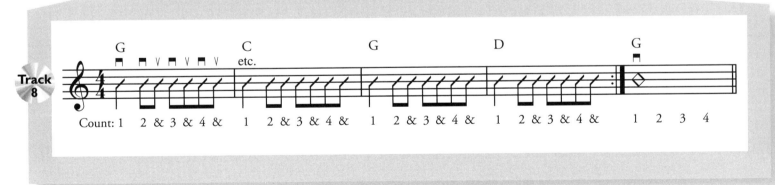

Black Haired Lady

Rhythm Builder: Ties and Dots

Sometimes, we want to add some interest to our rhythms by having notes ring longer than their normal value. There are two symbols that allow us to do this, the *tie* and the *dot*.

The Tie

Two notes connected by a tie ring out as if they were one note. You count both but only attack the first, letting it ring through the time of the second. Tied notes must be on the same line or space on the staff.

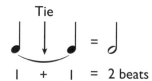

Beat value: 1   +   1   =   2 beats

> Two quarter notes tied together ring for the same duration as one half note.

The Dot

A dot to the right of a note adds half of the note's value to its duration.

Beat value: 1   +   ½   =   1½ beats

> This note is a *dotted quarter note*. It rings for 1½ beats.

Rhythm Builder: Syncopated Strumming

Before moving on to our next tune, let's learn a very useful strumming rhythm that uses ties to emphasize the offbeat. When a rhythm emphasizes an offbeat, it is *syncopated*. Syncopation is an important tool for creating rhythmic interest. Let's build this syncopated rhythm in steps:

1. First play this non-syncopated rhythm.

> The downstroke and upstroke symbols in parentheses (⊓) (∨) indicate where the pick passes over the strings without striking them.

2. Now, let's put a tie on the offbeat after beat 2. When you play this rhythm, your pick moves in a constant down-up motion but you pass over the strings as you strum the down stroke on beat three.

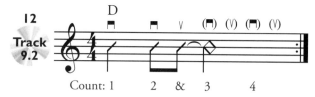

3. Finally we'll add some eighth notes to the end of the rhythm and you'll hear that the syncopation comes from purposely missing the strings on beat 3. Skipping the attack on the onbeat emphasizes the offbeat that comes before and after it.

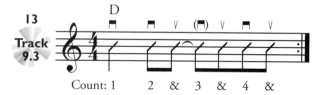

Lesson 2: Common Minor Chords in G

Some other chords that will come up often in the key of G are Emin (E Minor) and Amin. You are already familiar with Amin. Emin is a relatively easy chord to finger and has a smooth transition to and from the G chord. Learn the fingering for Emin below and try to find the consistencies it holds with G Major.

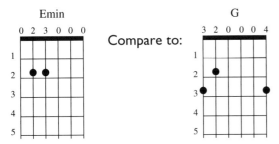

Once you recognize that the 2nd finger is in both Emin and G, try the example below. Keep that 2nd finger down as you change between the two chords.

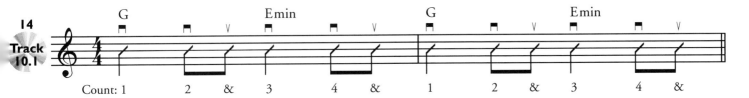

The next example gives you a chance to change between many chords. Before you start, analyze the chord changes. Look for similar fingering shapes and consistent fingers, so that you may take advantage of them when strumming the progression in time. Where there are no similarities, make the change as swiftly as possible in midair, keeping the constant down-up motion of your pick intact.

Changing in the Key of G

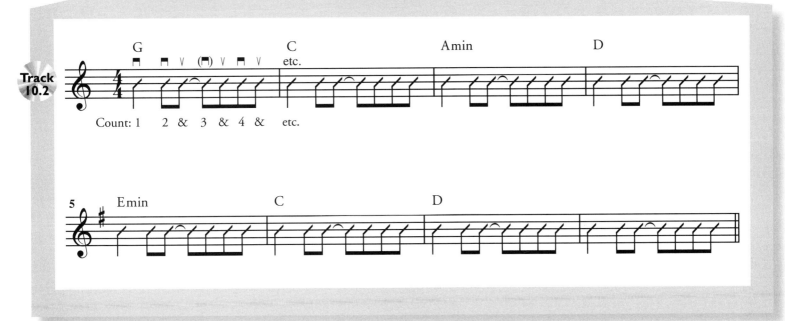

Combining Melody and Harmony

So far we've focused on chords. Chords are a kind of *harmony,* or notes that are sounded together. Another important characteristic of music is *melody.* Melody is usually easy to notice. It's in the forefront of the song, either sung by the vocalist or played on an instrument. If the guitar takes the melody it can be played on single strings or it can be harmonized with other strings or chords. Like chords, melodies come from the notes in a key.

A *key signature* (see pages 30–32), appearing at the beginning of each line of music, tells us which of the natural notes are altered by sharps or flats throughout the song. "A Friend of G" is in the key of G Major and uses F-sharp (F♯) instead of F-natural. Every key has a different key signature. (A chart of all the key signatures is on pages 31 and 32.)

Here's a tune that harmonizes a simple, descending melody in the key of G Major. Follow the left-hand fingering written below the TAB to set your fingers up for the chord strums between melody notes.

A Friend of G

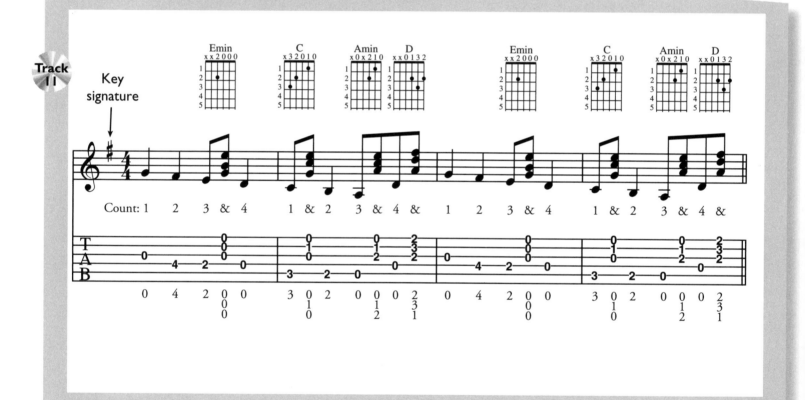

Sometimes we play short melodies between vocal lines, between chords or at the end of entire chord progressions. Guitarists call these short, melodic ideas *riffs* or *fills*.

Riff Builder: The Hammer-On

One trick we use to spice up our riffs or *licks* (short musical phrases usually played on the upper strings) is the *hammer-on*. We use it when we want two consecutive ascending notes to have a smooth, connected sound. To perform a hammer-on, attack the first note with the pick as normal. Sound the second note without using the pick by quickly pushing down on a string behind a fret and holding your finger there. The motion is similar to playing piano keys. The hammer-on is one type of *slur*, or non-attacked note change. Slurred notes are connected by a curved line that *looks* like a tie. But, remember that tied notes are on the same line or space of the staff (see page 20), while slurs occur between notes of different pitches and letter names. Try the example below.

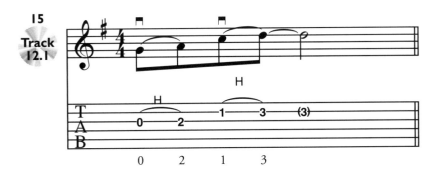

Here's a tune in the style of Bob Marley's "Redemption Song" that uses hammer-ons in a melodic opening written in standard music notation and TAB. The opening leads to a syncopated strumming section written in rhythmic notation. (See Rhythm Builder: Syncopated Strumming, page 20). This tune uses one new chord, G/B (fingering shown to the right), which is a slash chord (see page 18).

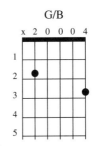

Song of Freedom

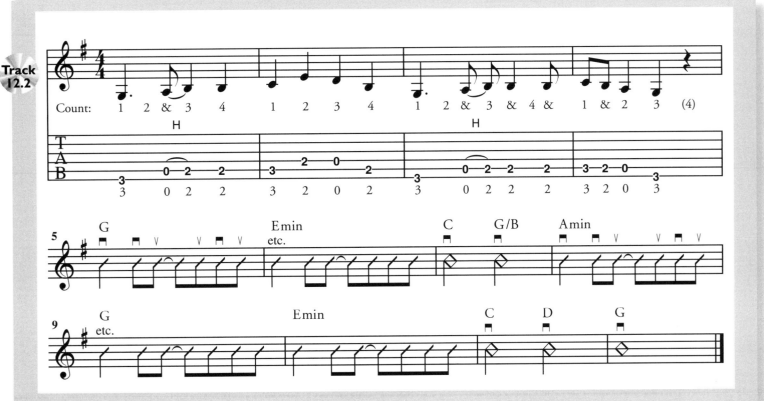

Lesson 3: The Primary Chords in D

Now, let's move to the key of D Major. To the right are this key's three primary chords.

You will often encounter an alternate fingering for G. In the key of D, this fingering facilitates changes between D, A and G. When changing these chords notice the consistent 3rd finger in both D and G. When changing to A, from D or G, just slide your 3rd finger to the 2nd fret without lifting it off the 2nd string. Changing between these chords will become easy if approached this way. Try it.

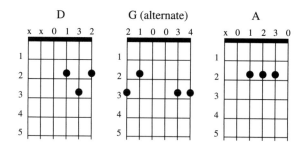

Rhythm Builder: Changing on the Offbeat

You can achieve a syncopated feel by occasionally changing chords on an offbeat. As this chord motion calls for quick shifts, you must focus on consistent fingers to perform these changes comfortably. Try this one.

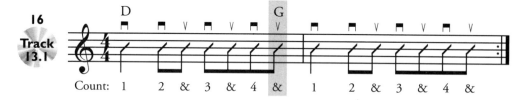

For an even more syncopated feel, try adding some ties. Don't forget to keep your constant down-up pick motion.

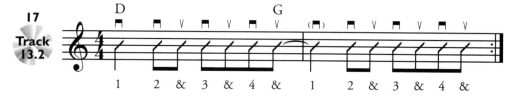

Riff Builder: The Pull-Off

A *pull-off* is basically the opposite of the hammer-on. As with the hammer-on, we use this slur when we want a smooth, connected sound. The difference is that hammers are used for going up (the notes A to B for example) and pull-offs are used for coming down (like B to A). To perform a pull-off, place a finger behind the fret of the higher note and the fret of the lower note at the same time. (Just place the higher note if the lower note is open). Now, attack the higher note with the pick as normal, then sound the lower note by lifting or pulling-off the higher finger. The lower note will sound clear and loud if your higher finger slightly plucks the string as it lifts off. Try this example.

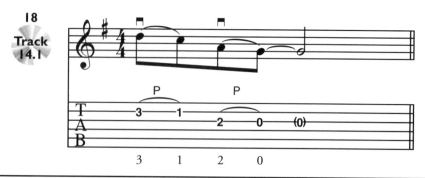

Here's a song in the key of D that uses chord changes on offbeats. Note that the F and C notes are always sharp in the key of D Major, as shown by the key signature. The G/D chord is easiest to finger if you keep your 3rd finger on the 2nd string.

"Carefree in D" repeats with a two different endings. In general, *1st and 2nd endings* are used with the repeat sign to add variation to otherwise repeated sections. Play to the repeat sign and repeat as normal, but on the second time through, skip over the music under the 1st bracket and play on from the 2nd bracket.

Carefree in D

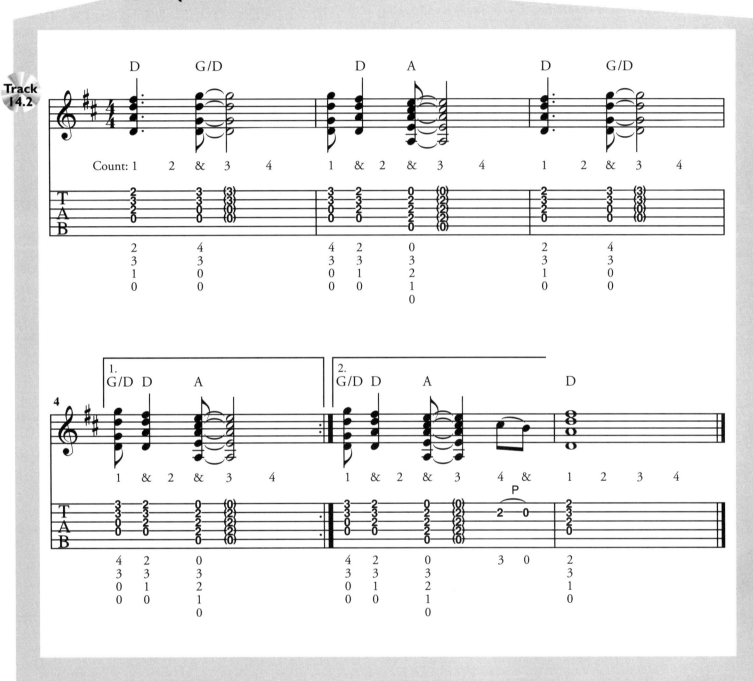

Lesson 4: The Primary Chords in C

The primary chords in the key of C are C, F and G. You already have experience with C and G; now we need to incorporate F. We'll start with slash-chord versions of F. Later in Chapter 5 (page 43), we'll use a full six-string F chord. To the right are two ways to play F.

Both of these slash chords use the four inside strings (2nd–5th). When you strum them, avoid the 6th and 1st strings. Practice changing from F/A to C, focusing on the consistent shape of your 2nd and 3rd fingers and without lifting your 1st finger. Also, try F/C to C and notice that your 1st and 3rd fingers stay in place for both chords.

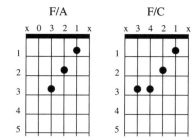

Rhythm Builder: Sixteenth Notes

Some rhythms use *sixteenth notes* to divide the beat into four parts instead of two. When a rhythm calls for sixteenth notes, we maintain our constant down-up pick motion, but now the onbeat and the offbeat fall on downstrokes. A measure filled with sixteenth notes is played and counted like this:

19

Track 15

Count: 1 e & ah 2 e & ah 3 e & ah 4 e & ah

Sixteenth notes look similar to eighth notes, but grouped sixteenth notes have two beams instead of one. Likewise, a single sixteenth note has two flags instead of one.

Single sixteenth note	Four sixteenth notes
= ¼ beat	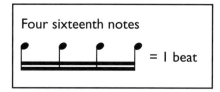 = 1 beat

Here's an example in the style of Cat Stevens' "Wild World." It gives you a chance to use the F/A chord, the bass-strum technique (see page 18), some slurs and a short melodic fill that uses all the notes in the key of C. Notice that beat 4 of the 2nd measure has two sixteenth notes and one eighth note beamed together. You'll see this sort of beaming often. Follow the picking as indicated to get a smooth, rhythmic flow.

Crazy Planet

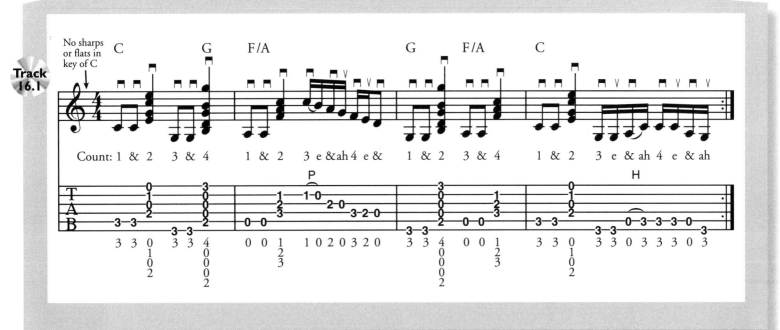

Now try this repeating chord progression. Folk guitarists, like Woody Guthrie or Bob Dylan, might repeat the music between two repeat signs a number of times to introduce a song or to tell a story. Watch out for the eighth note beamed to two sixteenth notes on beat four.

Rolling Rocks

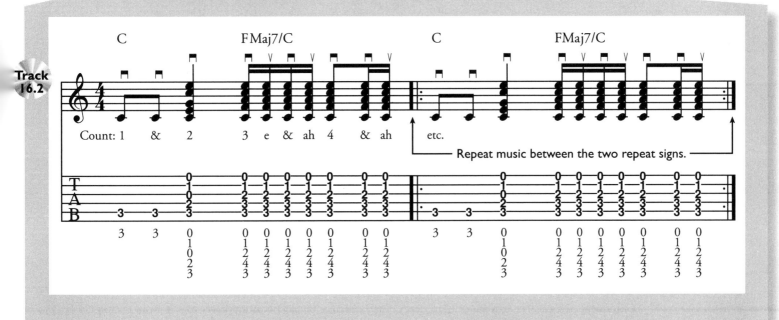

Lesson 5: Common Minor Chords in C

Amin, Emin and Dmin are three minor chords that appear in the key of C. You already know Amin and Emin. Take a look at the Dmin diagram to the right.

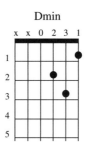

Try changing between Amin and Dmin. Notice that your 1st and 3rd fingers maintain a consistent diagonal shape in both chords.

Focus on this consistant diagonal shape as you change between chords.

The next example incorporates Amin, Dmin and Emin with chord changes on the offbeat. This tune starts with a *pickup*. A pickup is one or more notes that lead into the first full measure of a song. "Oldie but Goodie" starts with a pickup on beat 4. Notice how the counts of the last measure and the pickup add up to a full measure. To start the tune, count "one, two, three," and play on four.

Oldie but Goodie

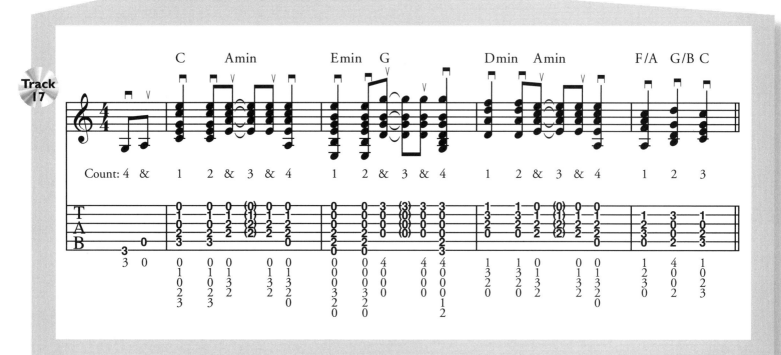

Chapter 4: Moving Around in the Key

In Chapter 3 (page 19), we used major and minor chords from three keys to play some songs. This chapter will thoroughly define keys and show you how scales and chords are constructed.

Lesson 1: The Major Scale

A *scale* is a set of pitches that are separated by a specific pattern of whole steps (W) and half steps (H). (See page 8 for an explanation of whole and half steps.) The *major scale* is most important to understand because we use it to define keys, build chords and construct melodies. It has seven different notes before it repeats itself. We find these notes by moving up the pattern, W–W–H–W–W–W–H, from any starting note. Completing this pattern once brings us back to the note name from which we started. Let's look at an example.

The scale below is the C Major scale, named after its starting note or *tonic*. We can start this pattern from 12 different pitches to build 12 different major scales. Each scale uses all seven letters of the musical alphabet only once before the scale repeats itself. The notes of the scale —from the lowest to highest—are given number names called *scale degrees*, which can also be labeled with the traditional syllables: do–re–mi–fa–sol–la–ti–do. The eighth scale degree (also called the *octave*) has the same letter name as the 1st scale degree but it is higher in pitch.

W = Whole step
H = Half step

The C Major Scale

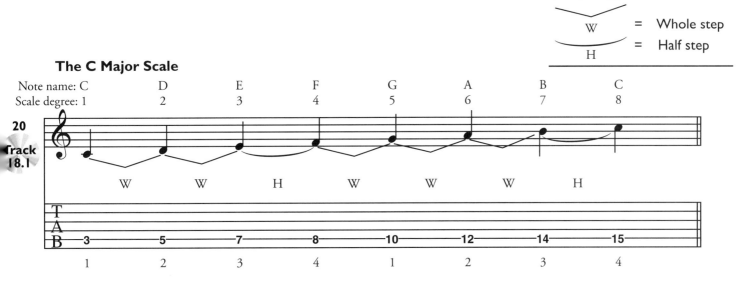

If we start the major scale on any note other than C, some notes will become sharp or flat to maintain the major scale pattern. Now, listen closely to the D Major scale as you play it up the 4th string. Notice that the D Major scale has two sharps, F♯ and C♯, yet it has the same "do–re–mi…" sound as the C Major scale.

The D Major Scale

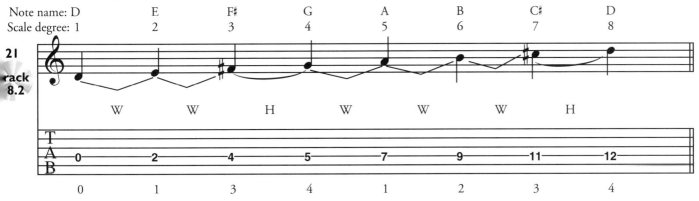

Key Signatures, Diatonic Notes and Accidentals

The seven notes in a major scale define a key because it is with these notes that we build the chords and melodies that fit in a key. To simplify reading and playing in keys, we use key signatures (placed at the beginning of each line of music) to remind us which notes of the scale remain sharp or flat. This way we don't have to see sharps or flats next to notes if they are *diatonic* (belonging to the scale).

If we do see a sharp (♯), flat (♭) or natural sign (♮) next to a note, it is outside of the key and the sign is called an *accidental*. Accidentals alter a note for the duration of a measure. Bar lines (page 13) cancel accidentals and return us to the key signature.

Usable Scale Fingerings

Here's a fingering for the C Major scale in the 1st position using open strings. (Compare this scale fingering to the melodic fill in "Crazy Planet" on page 27.)

Here's a *closed* fingering (one that uses only fretted notes) for the D Major scale in the 2nd position. Compare its shape with that of the C Major scale fingering above.

Here's an open fingering for the G Major scale in the 1st position. (Compare this fingering to the descending melody in "A Friend of G" on page 22.)

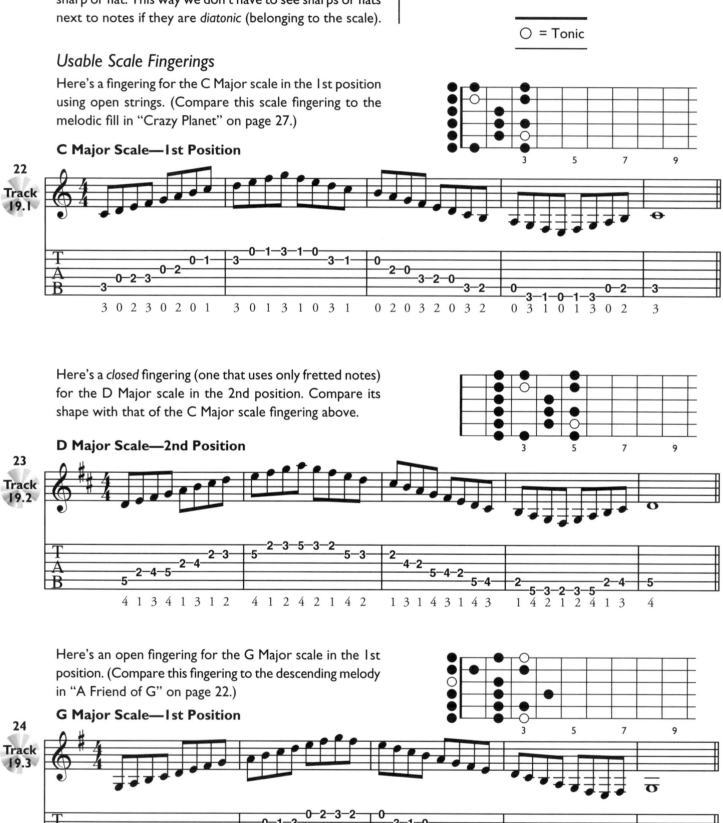

Here's a closed A Major scale fingering in the 2nd position. It follows the same shape as the G scale fingering on page 30. Note that this key has three sharps: F♯, C♯ and G♯. Also, note that your pinky must stretch one fret higher—out of position—on the 4th string. This is indicated by the plus sign (+) next to the left-hand fingering. Do your best with your pinky and don't sacrifice the good home-base positioning of your other three fingers.

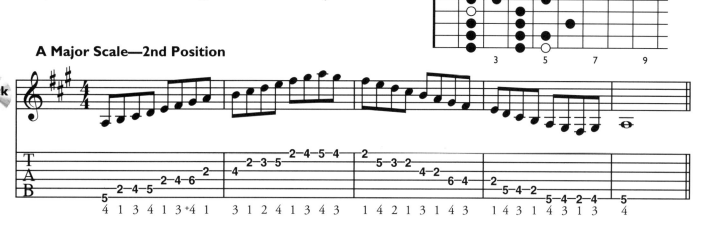

A Major Scale—2nd Position

25
Track
20

You can use the following diagrams as a reference for key signatures and notes of the major scales.

The Sharp Keys

The key of C is offered here for comparison, but remember that it has no sharps or flats in its key signature, so it is neither a sharp key or a flat key. The keys below, after C, take on sharp notes to maintain the W–W–H–W–W–W–H pattern of the major scale.

Key	Scale Degrees								Key Signature
	1	2	3	4	5	6	7	8	
Key of C	C	D	E	F	G	A	B	C	
Key of G	G	A	B	C	D	E	F♯	G	
Key of D	D	E	F♯	G	A	B	C♯	D	
Key of A	A	B	C♯	D	E	F♯	G♯	A	
Key of E	E	F♯	G♯	A	B	C♯	D♯	E	
Key of B	B	C♯	D♯	E	F♯	G♯	A♯	B	
Key of F♯	F♯	G♯	A♯	B	C♯	D♯	E♯	F♯	

The Flat Keys

The keys below, after C, take on flat notes to maintain the W–W–H–W–W–W–H pattern of the major scale.

Key	Scale Degrees								Key Signature
	1	2	3	4	5	6	7	8	
Key of C	C	D	E	F	G	A	B	C	
Key of F	F	G	A	B♭	C	D	E	F	
Key of B♭	B♭	C	D	E♭	F	G	A	B♭	
Key of E♭	E♭	F	G	A♭	B♭	C	D	E♭	
Key of A♭	A♭	B♭	C	D♭	E♭	F	G	A♭	
Key of D♭	D♭	E♭	F	G♭	A♭	B♭	C	D♭	
Key of G♭	G♭	A♭	B♭	C♭	D♭	E♭	F	G♭	

Diatonic Intervals

An interval is the distance between two pitches. Diatonic notes are easily related to the tonic of the scale by interval names. For example, the distance between the 1st and 2nd degree of a scale is called a 2nd, the distance between the 1st and 3rd degree is called a 3rd, and so on. Intervals also have a quality, or type of sound. Some diatonic intervals sound major (M) while others sound perfect (P). You can measure the interval between any two notes by counting up from the lower note as if it was the tonic of a key.

Diatonic Intervals of the C Major Scale

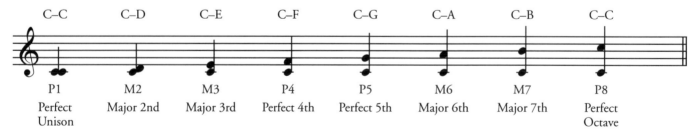

C–C	C–D	C–E	C–F	C–G	C–A	C–B	C–C
P1	M2	M3	P4	P5	M6	M7	P8
Perfect Unison	Major 2nd	Major 3rd	Perfect 4th	Perfect 5th	Major 6th	Major 7th	Perfect Octave

Non-Diatonic Intervals

When the upper note of a diatonic interval is lowered by a half step, the quality of the interval changes. Major intervals (M) become minor (m) and perfect intervals (P) become *diminished* (dim). Below are all the diatonic and non-diatonic intervals from the unison to the octave.

Diatonic and Non-Diatonic Intervals in the Key of C

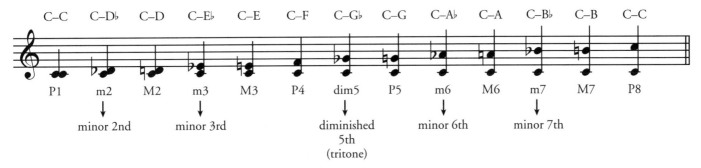

Lesson 2: Building Chords from the Major Scale

Now we'll use our knowledge of the major scale to build chords.

Triads

As said before, we use the major scale to find the chords that fit into a key. To do this, we use each scale degree as a root note for one of seven diatonic chords (chords from the key). We then add two notes above the root (the 3rd and 5th) to form a *triad*. A triad is three notes separated by the interval of a 3rd. When formed from a scale, triads will sound major, minor or diminished. Play this next example, listening carefully to the different qualities of the major, minor and diminished triads.

C Major Scale Harmonized with Triads

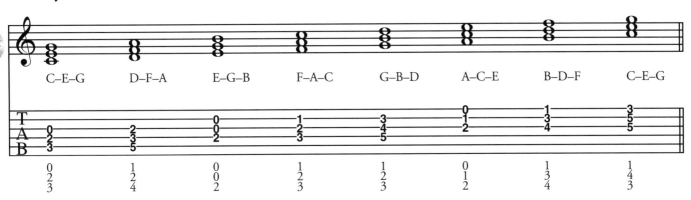

Triads are built in 3rds.	
C	C–D–E–F–G
Dmin	D–E–F–G–A
Emin	E–F–G–A–B
	etc.

Doubling Notes in the Triad

As briefly mentioned in Chapter 2 (page 15), chords are made up of three or more notes. Therefore, triads are chords. They provide the three notes needed to create a major, minor or diminished chord. Sometimes, entire guitar parts are based on three-string triads, but usually we reach for bigger sounding chord *voicings* that double some of the triad notes on other strings. A voicing is a particular arrangement, or fingering, of a chord. All the chords we've used in examples so far have consisted of the notes of the triads, with some of these notes doubled or even tripled.

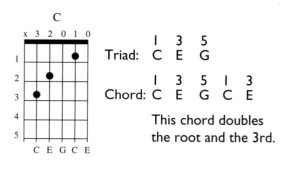

Triad:
I	3	5
C	E	G

Chord:
I	3	5	I	3
C	E	G	C	E

This chord doubles the root and the 3rd.

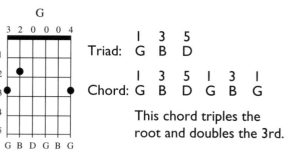

Triad:
I	3	5
G	B	D

Chord:
I	3	5	I	3	I
G	B	D	G	B	G

This chord triples the root and doubles the 3rd.

Roman Numerals

Chords, like scale degrees, can be labeled with numbers to show their relationship to the major scale. We label a chord with the roman numeral that coincides with the scale degree of the chord's root note. For example, C (1) = I, F (4) = IV, etc. This helps us distinguish chord labels from scale degree labels. We use upper case numerals for major chords and lower case numerals for minor chords. The seventh chord in the scale is diminished and is labeled with a lower case numeral and a circle (vii°).

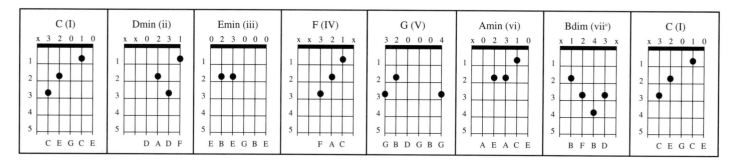

Roman Numeral Review

I or i	1	V or v	5
II or ii	2	VI or vi	6
III or iii	3	VII or vii	7
IV or iv	4		

Roman numerals help us understand and communicate how chords function in all keys.

For instance, in any major key:

- The I, IV and V are major chords. (These are the primary chords. See right; also see Chapter 3, page 19.)
- The ii, iii and vi are minor chords.
- The vii° is a diminished chord.

The Primary Chords

In Chapter 3, we talked a lot about the primary chords. They are the three most used chords in any key and have the 1st, 4th and 5th scale degrees as root notes. In major keys, they are always major chords and are labeled I, IV and V.

Now, let's use some more chords from the key of C. Here, we are also using the ii (Dmin) and iii (Emin). This song starts with the same repeated sequence as "Rolling Rocks" on page 27.

Back at Rolling Rocks

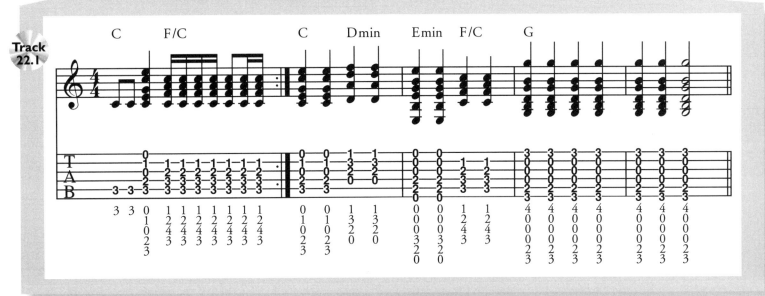

Track 22.1

Lesson 3: Minor Keys

Not all songs are in major keys. Some have a distinctly darker sound; this is the sound of a *minor key*. Minor keys are closely related to major keys, yet focus on different notes (and chords). In fact, any major scale becomes a minor scale if it "focuses"—or starts and ends—on the 6th scale degree instead of the 1st.

The Natural Minor Scale

The *natural minor scale* shares all the same notes with another major scale. The chart below shows how the notes of the C Major scale relate to the notes of the A Natural Minor scale.

Scale Notes	C	D	E	F	G	A	B	C	D	E	F	G	A
C Major Scale Degrees	1	2	3	4	5	6	7	8/1	2	3	4	5	6
A Minor Scale Degrees						1	2	♭3	4	5	♭6	♭7	8/1

If a song stays focused on the 6th degree of a major scale, we re-number the scale degrees so that what was the 6th degree in major becomes the 1st degree (tonic) in minor. Although the notes are the same, the relationship between them and the new tonic changes. If we compare the scale degrees of the natural minor scale to the scale degrees of its *parallel major scale* (the major scale with the same tonic as the minor scale, in this case A) the scale degrees for the natural minor scale become: 1–2–♭3–4–5–♭6–♭7.

Play and listen to the sound of this A Natural Minor scale below. Notice that, like C Major, the key of A Minor has no sharps or flats in its key signature. These keys are considered *relative*—*relative major* and *relative minor*—because they share the same key signature.

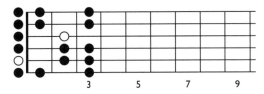

The A Minor Scale (Key of A Minor)

Track 2.2

Scale degrees: 1 2 ♭3 4 5 ♭6 ♭7 1   2 ♭3 4 5 ♭6 ♭7 ♭6 5   4 ♭3 2 1 ♭7 ♭6 5 4   ♭3 2 1 ♭7 ♭6 5 ♭6 ♭7   1

The Harmonic Minor Scale

A common variation on the minor scale is the *harmonic minor scale*. This scale has a natural 7th scale degree (as opposed to the flat 7th of the natural minor scale). The scale degrees of the harmonic minor scale are: 1–2–♭3– 4–5–♭6–7. Play the scale below and listen for the 1½ step leap between the ♭6th and 7th scale degrees.

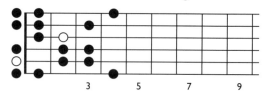

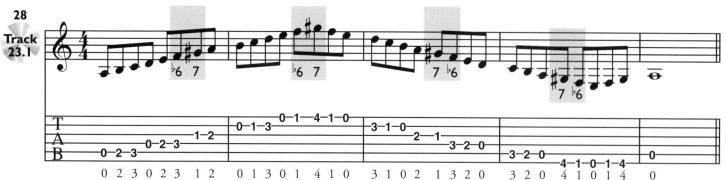

The Primary Chords in Minor Keys

We generally use the harmonic minor scale to build triads and chords in the minor keys. When we build our seven diatonic chords from each scale degree of the harmonic minor scale, these chords are labeled with roman numerals as they are in major key, but have different qualities. What was I and IV in major, becomes i and iv in minor. The V will usually remain as V (although it will sometimes appear as v).

Labeling chords in a minor key is not as simple as with a major key. This is due to the variations on the minor scale. However, this can make minor tunes more interesting because they offer a songwriter a lot of room for creativity and can take the listener by surprise. Below are versions of the i, iv and V as they often appear in the key of A Minor.

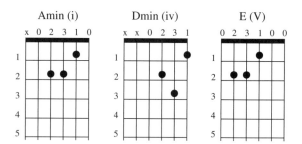

Rhythm Builder: Grace Notes

Sometimes, notes are preceded by quick, ornamental notes ♪ that have no rhythmic value of their own. These uncounted, quick notes are called *grace notes*. A grace note appears in music as a tiny note next to the normal sized note that it embellishes. Often, the grace note is slurred to the note it preceeds. Remembering the introduction to "Song of Freedom" on page 23, try this opening riff that uses grace notes in place of counted hammer-ons.

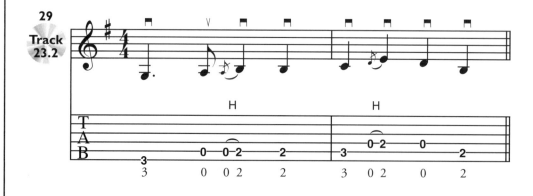

Riff Builder: The Slide

The *slide* is yet another slur. This one connects both ascending and descending pairs of notes. To produce a slide you must attack a note and, without taking pressure off the string, slide your finger to a higher or lower note. As you slide, keep even pressure on the string and look ahead to the fret to which you are sliding. You will need to execute slides in different ways. Compare the sound and notation of the examples below. Example 30 slurs together two notes of countable duration, while example 31 starts with a grace note that ornaments or embellishes the second note.

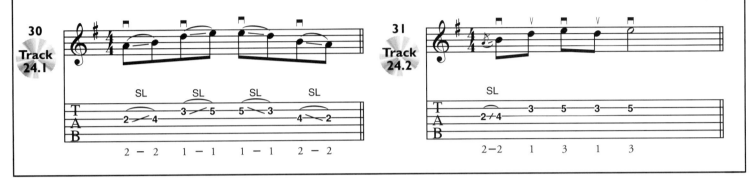

Riff Builder: The Bend

The *bend* is a slur that changes the pitch of a fretted note by pushing up or pulling down on the fretted string until it becomes a new note. On the acoustic guitar, we can bend the pitch of a string up a half step *(half-step bend)* or a whole step *(whole-step bend)*. Using the bend, we can also make a change in pitch that is smaller than a half step (which is not otherwise possible). A slight bend such as this is called a *quarter-step bend*. Bends can be challenging on an acoustic guitar due to string tension. It is usually helpful to use the strength of multiple fingers to perform a bend. Placing your free fingers behind the fretted note can actually help push (or pull) on the string. This will make it easier to successfully alter the string's pitch.

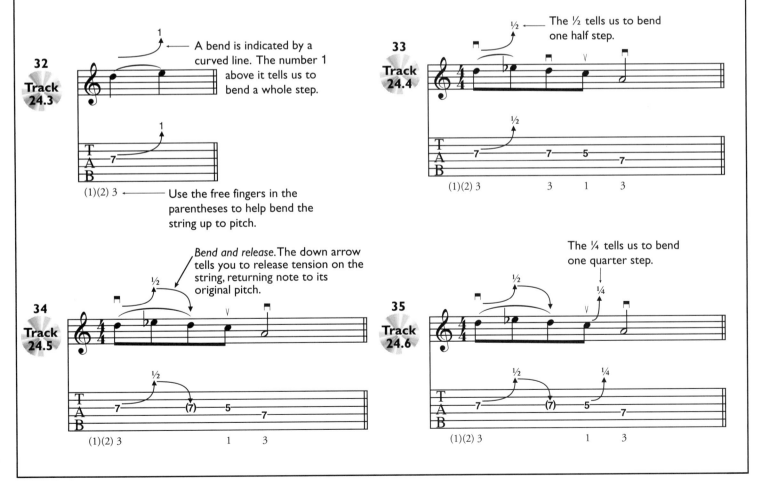

Here's a tune that uses primary chords in the key of A Minor. It also features many fill riffs that utilize different slur techniques.

She Left Me Dim

Track 25

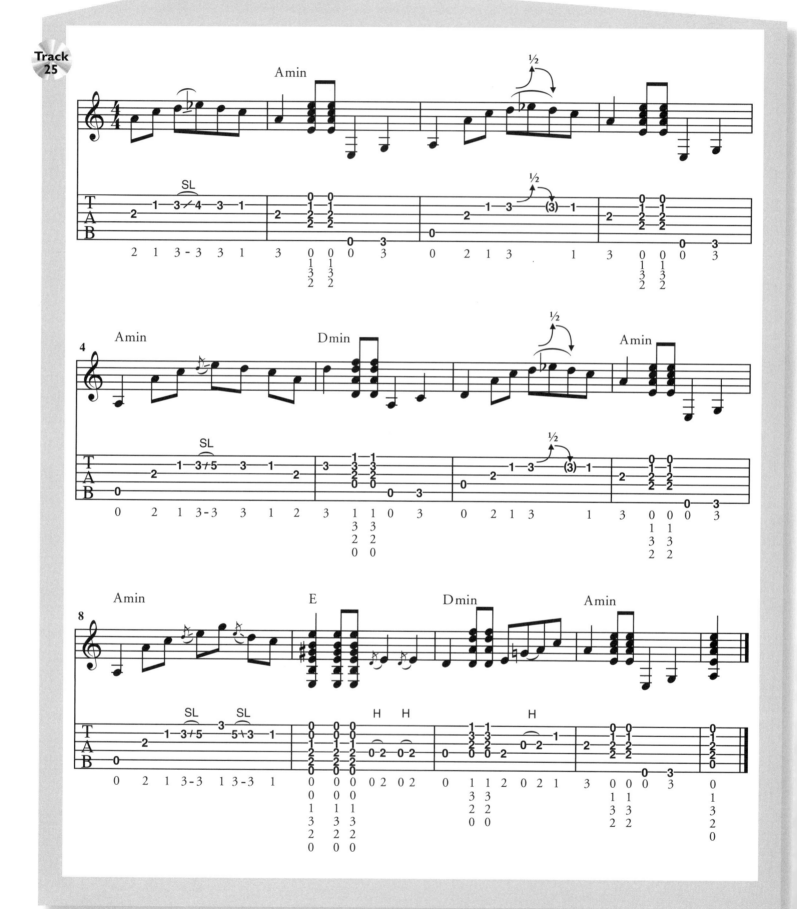

Chapter 5: More on Chords

In Chapter 4, we discussed scales and keys, and how they are used to construct chords. The chords we've used in our songs so far have been triads with doubled (or tripled) notes. There are hundreds of great songs that use progressions made solely of diatonic triads. Yet, sometimes, for a less predictable sound, we add notes to our chords other than the notes of the triad. We can even alter our chords with notes that are outside the key or insert non-diatonic chords to produce tension in the music. This chapter deals with changing chord qualities (major to minor), movable forms of major and minor chords and the use of 7th chords. All of these concepts will spice up your chord playing and prepare you for later chapters.

Lesson 1: Making Major Chords Minor

On page 33, we described triads as three notes separated by the interval of a 3rd. Another way to find the notes of a triad is by taking the 1st, 3rd and 5th degrees of the major scale. For instance, look again at the D Major scale (to the right).

Notice that D and F♯ are separated by a 3rd (E is between them), just as F♯ and A are separated by a third (G is between them). If we play these three notes, we hear the sound of a major triad. Therefore, we can say that a major triad is spelled from the 1st, 3rd, and 5th scale degrees of the major scale.

To change the quality of a triad from major to minor all you need to do is lower the 3rd scale degree by one half step. So, a D Minor triad is spelled: D–F–A.

D Major Scale

Scale Note	D	E	F♯	G	A	B	C♯	D
Scale Degree	1	2	3	4	5	6	7	8/1

D Major Triad

Major Triad Spelling	D	F♯	A
Scale Degree	1	3	5

D Minor Triad

Minor Triad Spelling	D	F	A
Scale Degree	1	♭3	5

A ♭ in front of a scale degree tells us that the scale note has been lowered a half step.

We've already played major and minor versions of chords that share the same root note. Comparing the chord diagrams below, notice that only one note changes when you change from a major chord to a minor chord of the same root note (even though the fingering may be very different).

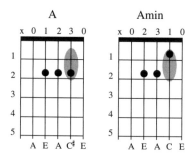
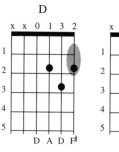
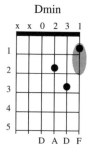
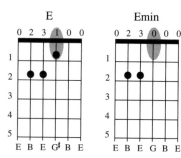

The fingerings we've learned for C and G are not as easy to make into minor chords. This is because these fingerings double the 3rd scale degree (see page 34, Doubling Notes in the Triad) and we quickly run out of fingers when we try to lower notes on two strings. The next lesson provides a solution to this problem.

Lesson 2: Movable Barre Chords

All the chords we've played in previous lessons (excluding F/C and Bdim) are referred to as *open chords* because at least one note of the chord is played on an open string. Since some keys call for chords that we cannot finger as open chords, we need to learn fingerings that do not use open strings. These fingerings are called *closed* or *movable chords*. When you move a closed fingering up to different neck positions, the quality (major, minor or diminished) doesn't change, while the root note of the chord does.

Now, let's learn two movable chord forms. One is based on the open E chord shape and has its root note on the 6th string. The other is based on the open A chord shape and has its root note on the 5th string. To form these chords we must use our 1st finger to fret notes on more than one string at the same fret at the same time. This technique is called a *barre*.

⌒ A barre is indicated by a curved line.

Moveable Barre Chords with the Root Note on the 6th String

In a few steps, let's transform the open E chord into a movable chord shape that has its root note on the 6th string. (The root of the chord is indicated by a hollow dot ○ in the diagrams that follow.)

1. Finger an open E chord.

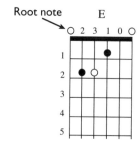

2. Now, rearrange your fingers so that your 1st is replaced by your 2nd, your 2nd is replaced by your 3rd, and your 3rd is replaced by your 4th. This leaves your 1st finger free, hovering beyond the nut.

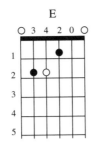

E

3. Next, keeping intact the shape of your 2nd, 3rd and 4th fingers, move your entire hand to the 3rd position. (Remember that your 1st finger determines your position.)

4. Lay your 1st finger flat across all six strings (close to the 3rd fret) and press down. This is called a barre. Try to distribute the pressure of the barre as evenly as possible across the strings without changing the setup of your other fingers. Finally, strum this movable chord fingering. When lined up to the 3rd fret, this chord's root note is G, therefore it's called a G Major barre chord.

G

5. Try moving the G barre chord form a whole step higher. You'll notice that the major quality of the chord remains, but the chord changes its root and becomes an A Major barre chord.

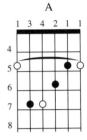

A

Movable Barre Chords with the Root Note on the 5th String

Now, let's transform the open A chord shape into a movable barre chord with its root note on the 5th string.

1. First, finger an open A chord.

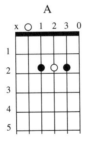

A

2. Now, rearrange your fingers so that you 1st finger is free. Like with the E chord above, your 1st finger is replaced by your 2nd, your 2nd is replaced by your 3rd, and so on.

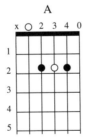

A

3. Next, keeping their shape, shift your 2nd, 3rd and 4th fingers to the 5th fret.

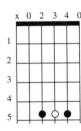

4. With your 1st finger, lay a barre on the 3rd fret across five strings (not the 6th string). This puts the chord shape in the 3rd position. Finally, strum this chord. This is a C Major barre chord with its root on the 5th string.

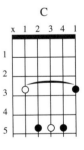

C

5. Try moving the fingering a whole step higher. Notice again that the major quality of the chord remains, but the chord changes its root and becomes D.

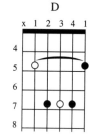

6. Here's an alternate fingering for a major barre chord with the root on the 5th string. In this fingering, the barre is played by the 3rd finger (not the 1st) and we purposely avoid the 1st string with the pick when strumming.

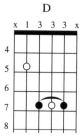

We can make these barre forms minor by lowering the 3rd of the chord, as we did for the open chords in the last lesson. The minor chords below are also movable since they do not use open strings. Here's a way to make G and C chords minor.

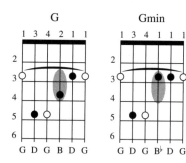
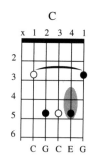
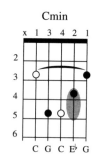

These barre chords allow us to play major and minor chords of any letter name, just by lining the form up to a desired root note.

Here's a barre-chord rhythm that uses sixteenth-note strumming. Keep a steady sixteenth-note strumming motion, even when not sounding the strings.

The Creepy Bar

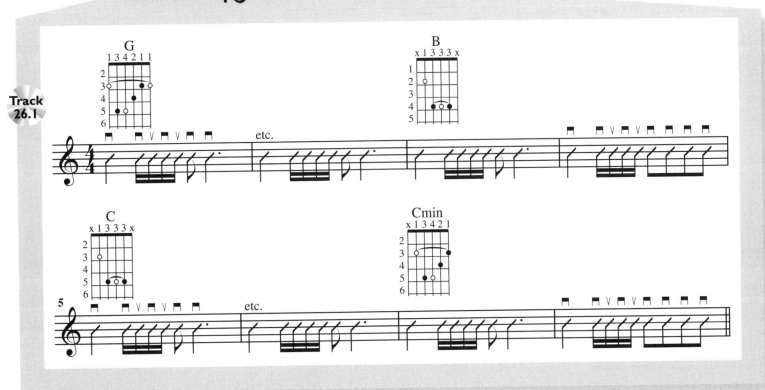

You may have heard Led Zeppelin or Dire Straits use barre chords like this to create a rhythmic backdrop for a monster rock solo.

Winding Down the Road

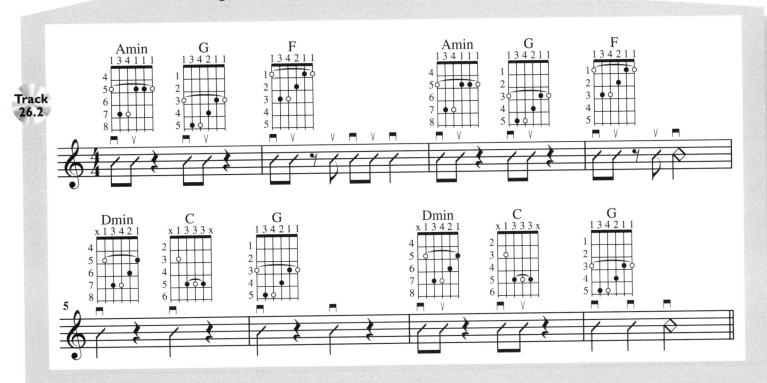

Lesson 3: 7th Chords

7th chords are four-note chords comprised of a triad and a 7th above the chord's root. Triads and 7ths of different qualities combine to create different types of 7th chords. The diagrams below demonstrate the possible combinations. Try these movable 7th chords.

M7 = Major 7th
m7 = Minor 7th

Root on 5th String | Root on 6th String

C Major 7th

C	E	G	B
1	3	5	7

└ Major Triad ┘
└───── M7 ─────┘

CMaj7

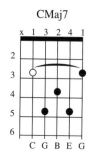

CMaj7

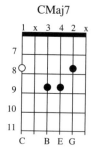

C Dominant 7th

C	E	G	B♭
1	3	5	♭7

└ Major Triad ┘
└───── m7 ─────┘

C7

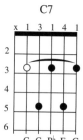

C7

C Minor 7th

C	E♭	G	B♭
1	♭3	5	♭7

└ Minor Triad ┘
└───── m7 ─────┘

Cmin7

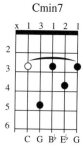

Cmin7

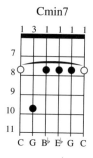

C Minor 7th ♭5

C	E♭	G♭	B♭
1	♭3	♭5	♭7

└ Dim Triad ┘
└───── m7 ─────┘

Cmin7♭5

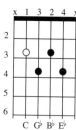

Cmin7♭5

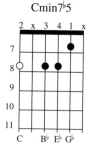

Diatonic 7th Chords

If we build a 7th chord off of each scale degree of the major scale, we would get the arrangement of diatonic 7th chords below. The upper row of chord diagrams features 7th chords in the open position (with the exception of Bmin7♭5). They are new forms, but are based on the diatonic triads on page 34. The lower row features the movable 7th chord fingerings we covered on page 44. Notice the Roman numeral for the Bmin7♭5 chord (vii∅). The circle with the diagonal slash ∅ indicates that this chord is a *half-diminished* chord. This type of chord consists of scale degrees: 1–♭3–♭5–♭7.

Open Position Diatonic 7th Chords

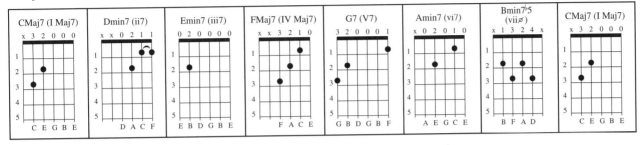

Movable Diatonic 7th Chords

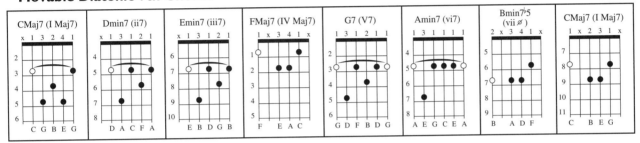

The Dominant 7th Chord

The dominant 7th chord is indicated by V7 in roman numerals. It appears in a key only once and is built on the 5th scale degree. Of the 7th chords above, the dominant 7th chord is the most prominent in music because it creates a tense sound that resolves most naturally when it moves to the tonic (I) chord of the key. The tension that the V7 creates helps define the key because our ears hear the resolution to the I chord as a return "home." A V7 can resolve to a major I chord of a major key as well as a minor i chord of a minor key.

Below are some V7 to I (or i) resolutions using mostly open chords.

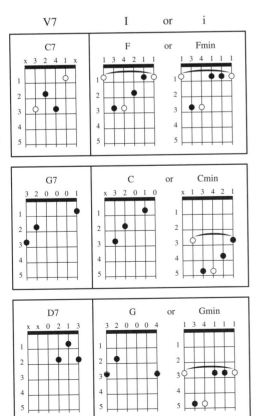

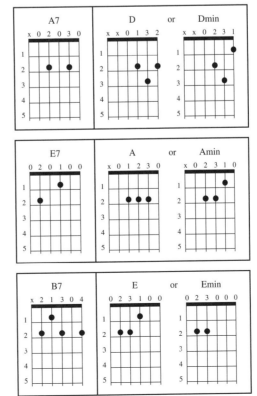

Rhythm Builder: The Eighth-Note Triplet

Our examples so far have used eighth notes and sixteenth notes, which divide the beat into two and four even parts, respectively. If we want to divide the beat into three parts we must use *eighth-note triplets*. This type of triplet looks like three eighth notes beamed together with the number *3* above or below the beamed group.

The three eighth notes of the triplet collectively have the duration of one beat. Eighth-note triplets consist of three eighth notes in the time of two.

Eighth-note triplet

$\prod_3$ = I Beat

Triplets can be tricky because they alter the flow of our pick motion. Familiarize yourself with the three pick motions below, as different ways to attack eighth-note triplets will come in handy for different pieces.

Pick Motion 1

36
Track 27.1

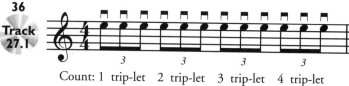

Count: 1 trip-let 2 trip-let 3 trip-let 4 trip-let

Pick Motion 2

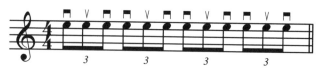

Pick Motion 3

Pick Motion 3 keeps a constant down-up pick motion, but watch out, this approach puts an upstroke on every *other* onbeat.

Rhythm Builder: Swing 8ths

Some eighth-note rhythms we encounter are performed with a slight "bounced" feel. Instead of even, or *straight* eighth notes (the way we've played eighth notes up to this point), these *swing eighths (Swing 8ths)* have a long-short sound. This sound is written one way and played another.

A measure that is played and counted like this (using the triplet feel):

37
Track 27.2

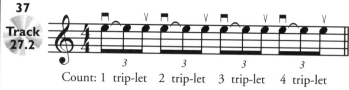

Count: 1 trip-let 2 trip-let 3 trip-let 4 trip-let

is written like this:

38
Track 27.3

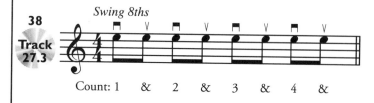

Count: 1   &   2   &   3   &   4   &

When the swing-eighth rhythm is called for, *Swing 8ths* will appear at the beginning of the music. You may also see this indication:

$\prod$ = $\prod_3$

Borrowed Chords

There is only one V7 chord and one tonic chord in a key, but some progressions "tonicize" other major or minor chords in the key; that is, they make them temporarily sound like a tonic or the "home chord." A major or minor chord that is not the tonic will sound like a tonic if preceded by a dominant 7th chord that is a 5th above its root note. (For example: If we are in the key of C and want to make Dmin—the ii chord—our temporary tonic, we would play the dominant 7th chord whose root note is a 5th above D; that chord is A7.) This dominant seventh chord is non-diatonic; it is *not* in the key of the song, but, it is borrowed from the key of the temporary tonic that is precedes. A dominant 7th chord used this way is called a *secondary dominant*.

Try this chord progression in the style of Arlo Guthrie's "Alice's Restaurant." The borrowed chords below are labeled with V7 followed by a slash and the roman numeral of the chord to which the secondary dominant resolves (for example: V7/ii). A symbol such as V7/ii is read "five seven of two." Listen carefully to the CD track before playing this tune as it is played with the swing eighths feel.

Red Hot Restaurant

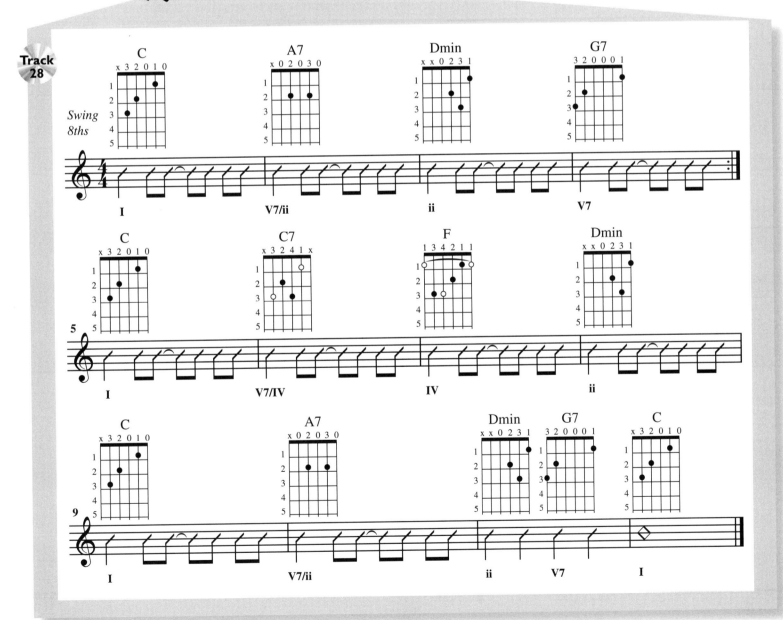

Chapter 6: Songs in Fingerstyle

This chapter will get you acquainted with *fingerstyle* technique. Fingerstyle, also know as *fingerpicking,* is a right-hand technique in which the thumb and fingers are used to pick the strings instead of a flatpick. Some guitarists fingerpick with their fingertips (or fingernails), while others like to slip on some fingerpicks and/or a thumb pick. The skills you learn in this chapter have been employed by performers and groups like Jewel, CSNY, John Prine, Tracy Chapman, Dan Folgelberg and many others to effectively support their song lyrics. In later chapters, we'll discuss some more complex fingerstyle techniques.

Lesson 1: Home Base for the Right Hand

The fastest way to get comfortable with your right hand is to assign each finger to a specific string. We'll call this assignment *home base.* When reading fingerstyle parts, you will see the traditional letters *p, i, m,* and *a* next to notes. These letters tell you which right-hand fingers you should use to pick the notes.

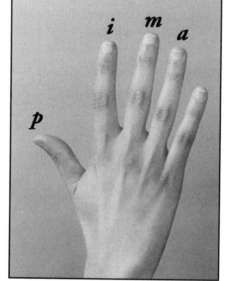

Right-hand fingers.

p	=	thumb
i	=	index finger
m	=	middle finger
a	=	ring finger

Let's get used to this assignment by picking across the notes of an Emin chord. When you play the notes of a chord in succession like this (rather than at the same time) it is called an *arpeggio.* Before you start, rest your thumb (*p*) gently on the 6th string. Then, rest your index (*i*), middle (*m*) and ring (*a*) fingers on the 3rd, 2nd and 1st strings, respectively. Your fingers are now resting on the strings they are assigned to pluck. The only exception is that your thumb must alternate between the 6th, 5th and 4th strings. Now that your fingers are in position, give the arpeggio a try.

E Minor Arpeggio Warm-Up

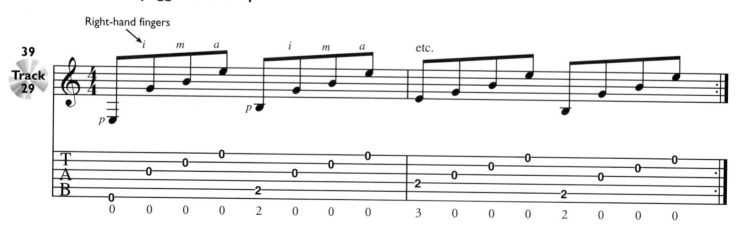

Lesson 2: Multi-Part Writing

Fingerstyle guitar makes it possible to provide bass, harmony and melody all at once. The next exercise is an example of two parts written on one staff. It uses slash chords to create a bass line independent of the arpeggios played on the higher strings. Notice that the bass notes, written with the stems pointing down, add up to an entire measure worth of beats. This is the *lower voice*. The eighth notes with the stems pointing up also fill the four-beat measure (include the rests). These make up the *upper voice*.

Bass, Gotta Add You

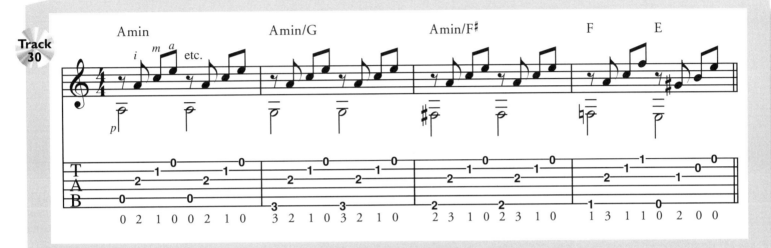

Let's take a moment to learn some other time signatures so we can try other interesting arpeggio examples.

Rhythm Builder: More Time Signatures

Songs can pulse in other groups of beats, beside the four in a measure of $\frac{4}{4}$ time. Two other common time signatures are $\frac{3}{4}$ and $\frac{6}{8}$. When we see time signatures (sometimes called *meters*) at the beginning of a piece, this is what they are telling us.

4 = The top number tells us that there are **four beats per measure**.
4 = The bottom number tells us that the quarter note duration gets the beat.

3 = The top number tells us that there are **three beats per measure**.
4 = The bottom number tells us that the quarter note duration gets the beat.

6 = The top number tells us that there are **six beats per measure**.
8 = The bottom number tells us that the eighth note duration gets the beat.

All of these time signatures give songs very different feels. The time signature $\frac{3}{4}$ is sometimes called *waltz time*, after the waltz dance that is always accompanied by music in this time signature. The time signature $\frac{6}{8}$ is used for the common "jig." This is distinct because it is a *compound meter*, which means that the individual eighth note beats naturally group together in two groups of three to give the measure a two-beat pulse. The arpeggios on page 50 demonstrate the feel of the $\frac{3}{4}$ and $\frac{6}{8}$ time signatures.

Try this picking pattern in ¾ time. Count aloud and give a slight accent to the onbeats. This will help you get the waltz feel (see Rhythm Builder, page 49). Also note the left-hand fingering. When fingerpicking, you don't always need to fret all the notes of a chord. It makes it easier to fret only the strings needed for the picking pattern.

> = Accent. Emphasize or play note louder than the others.

Waltz-Time Blues

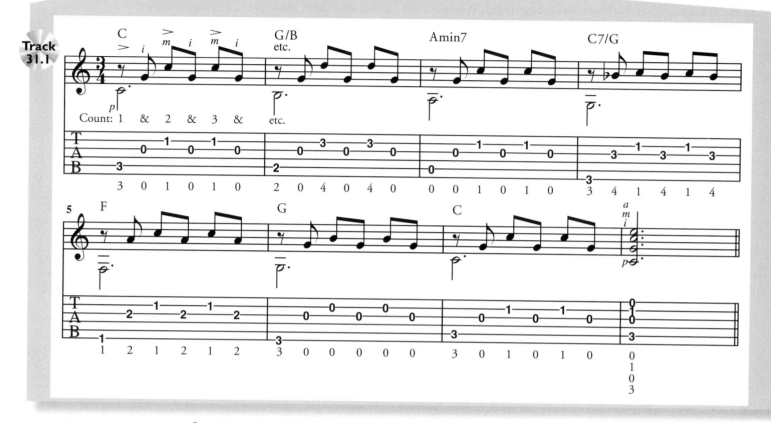

The next pattern is in ⁶⁄₈ time. You can count it in a "six" feel (1–2–3–4–5–6) or a "two" feel (as indicated in the music below). The larger numbers of the count (shown below) indicate the parts of the beats that should receive slight accents.

Rising Bass

This pattern is in the style of Fleetwood Mac's "Landslide" and is in $\frac{4}{4}$ time. Notice there are shared notes between the upper and lower voices (as indicated by two stems attached to one note). To make it easier to change between chords, leave your 1st finger down throughout this example.

Avalanche

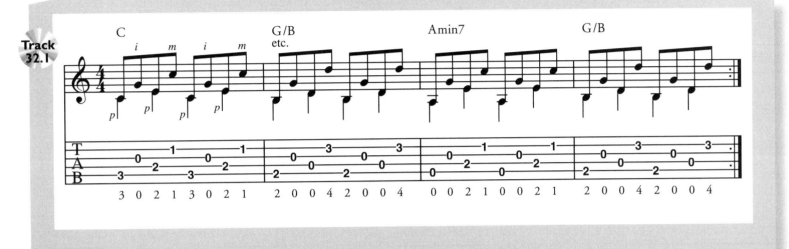

Playing Voices Together

Fingerstyle makes it easy to simultaneously play notes that are not on adjacent strings. Usually, this action is coordinated between a downstroke of the thumb and an upstroke of a finger. This technique is sometimes known as a *pinch*.

The example below utilizes this pinch technique on the first beat of each measure. When you attack the two notes, your thumb should move downward, away from your palm, while your finger moves upward toward your palm. After picking, release the tension in your fingers and get ready to strike again.

Stoppin' on One

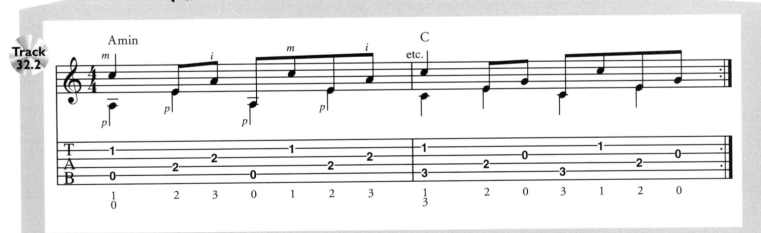

Melody and Non-Chord Tones

"Dusk with a Light Breeze" (on page 52) adds a melody to an upper voice. A melody may occasionally move to notes that are not part of the chord. These notes, called *non-chord tones*, can occur in the upper voice without changing the chord's name. They simply create a little tension and make the melody sound more independent of the harmony. Listen for the melody in this example.

Dusk with a Light Breeze

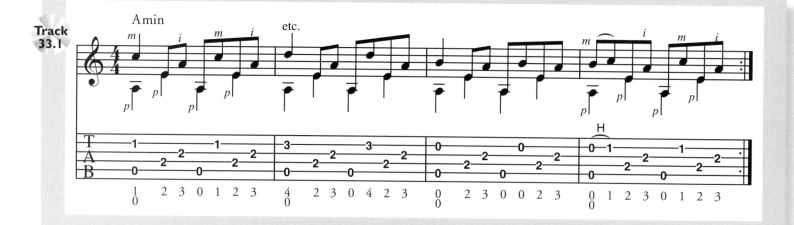

Track 33.1

Lesson 3: The Capo

A *capo* is a device that changes the pitch of the guitar strings. It clamps onto the neck of the guitar and functions like a movable nut. You can use the capo for a number of reasons. For one, it allows you to play a chord sequence in *any* key, using the *same* fingerings. This is extremely helpful when your intricate multi-part guitar arrangement doesn't work well for the range of your vocalist. In this case, you slap a capo on a higher fret, play your worked-out fingerings as if the capo was the guitar nut, and suddenly the key is just right for the vocalist to sing. Another reason to use the capo is to change the sound of your guitar. The higher up the neck you place the capo, the brighter the sound of the strings.

Once you have a capo, try the example below. Place the capo behind the 7th fret and play the notes at the frets indicated by the TAB. Following the fingerings below the TAB, you'll find that any note at the 7th fret is now an open note. A note at the 9th fret is written as 2nd fret, etc. If some of the notes produce a buzzing sound, try moving the capo closer to the 7th fret.

Rest Stop

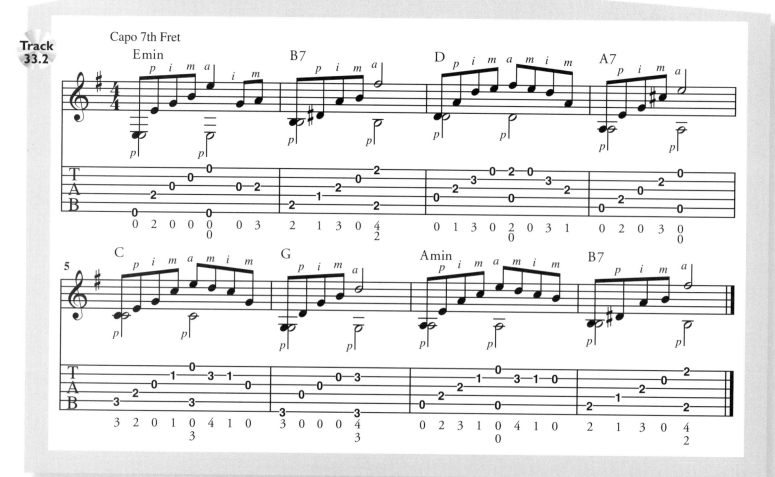

Track 33.2

PART 2: Acoustic Styles

Chapter 7: Bluegrass, Country and Folk Flatpicking

This chapter is devoted to the traditional "roots" flatpick styles made famous by pioneers like Jimmie Rodgers, Woody Guthrie, Lester Flatt and Doc Watson. These techniques have been honored and expanded by countless acoustic guitarists from the 1960s to the present day. The music of Nitty Gritty Dirt Band, The Weavers, Neil Young, Jerry Garcia (to name a few) is filled with creative embellishments of traditional flatpicking.

Lesson 1: Alternating Bass

One of the most characteristic features of "roots" rhythm playing is the *alternating bass*. In *strings bands* (groups who play music on stringed instruments such as guitar, banjo, mandolin, etc.), the guitarist often has a threefold job: 1) strumming the chords, 2) keeping the beat, and, 3) picking a bass line. All this is possible by using an modified version of the bass-strum technique (see Chapter 2, page 18). We still play single bass notes on the strong beats (usually beats 1 and 3, while we strum the upper parts of the chord on beats 2 and 4), but now the bass alternates between the root, 3rd and 5th of the chord. Let's take a look at what can be done in a few keys that are often used in bluegrass music: G, C and D.

This bluegrass tune below alternates between the root, 3rd and 5th in the bass. Watch out for the D chord. Here we stray from our left-hand home base positioning and hook our thumb over the neck to grab the 3rd of the chord (F#). The musical reason for straying from home base is that it allows us to keep notes ringing longer and to hold down our consistent 3rd finger.

Alternating Bass in G

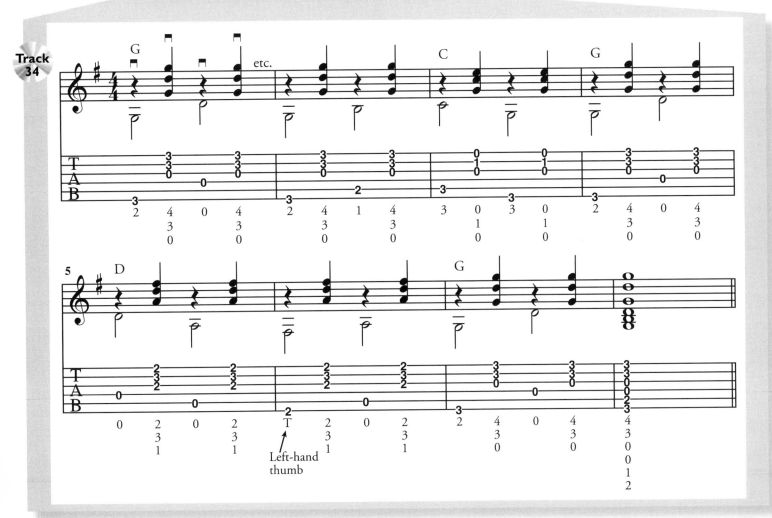

This rhythm part uses a similar bass line on the D chord as "Alternating Bass in G" (page 53). Note the slurs in measures 3 and 6. It is common in this style to embellish the bass line with hammer-on slurs.

Alternating Bass in D

For our alternating bass rhythm in the key of C, we'll change the feel to waltz time. Waltz time, or $\frac{3}{4}$ time, is described on page 49. Notice that the hammer-on embellishments are executed as grace notes.

Alternating Bass in C

Lesson 2: Diatonic Bass Fills

In Lesson 1 (page 53), we added interest to the I–IV–V chord progression by using chord notes, other than the root, to move the bass. Now, we'll further flesh out our bass parts by inserting fills (riffs) between chords. In this lesson, we'll use ascending and descending diatonic runs that smoothly connect two chords. These diatonic fills come from the five-note *major pentatonic scale*. This scale is the same as the major scale, but without the 4th and 7th scale degrees. Using only the 1st, 2nd, 3rd, 5th and 6th, the major pentatonic scale creates a versatile, open-ended sound that works well over chord progressions in many contexts. Try it ascending the 5th string.

The C Major Pentatonic Scale

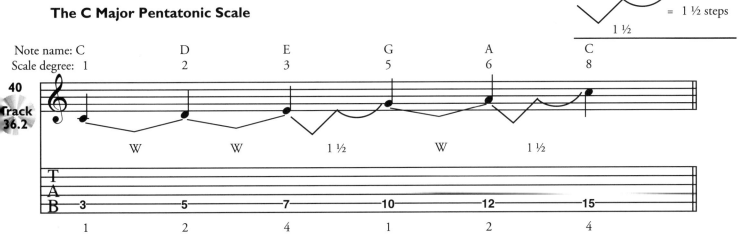

Usable Major Pentatonic Scale Fingerings

Below is the C Major Pentatonic scale in the 1st position. (Compare it to the C Major scale fingering on page 30.)

C Major Pentatonic Scale—1st Position

41 Track 37.1

This scale follows the shape or contour of the one above. However, it's a movable fingering in the 2nd position with D as its tonic.

D Major Pentatonic Scale—2nd Position

42 Track 37.2

Now, let's play a G Major Pentatonic scale in the 1st position.

G Major Pentatonic Scale—1st Position

43 Track 37.3

Alright, now we'll rearrange the fingering of the above scale so that it becomes a movable fingering. In this case, we move it to the 2nd position, which makes A its tonic.

A Major Pentatonic Scale—2nd Position

44 Track 37.4

With alternating bass and fingerings for the major scale and major pentatonic scale under your belt, you are ready to play a song with diatonic bass fills. Notice that the song ends on a dominant 7th chord instead of a regular tonic chord. This colorful technique of ending on a dominant 7th occurs often in country, bluegrass, jazz and blues styles. Bluegrass and country tunes, such as the one below, are often played with a swing eighths feel (see page 46).

Walkin' to the Changes

Lesson 3: Adding "Blues" to Fills

"Walking to the Changes" (page 57) ended on the bluesy sound of a C7 chord in place of C Major (the I or tonic). As we learned in Chapter 4 (pages 45), we (diatonically) would never see a dominant 7th chord built off the tonic of a key. But, in fact, there are frequent occurrences of such bluesy effects in bluegrass, country and other genres that have been influenced by blues. One way to create the "blues effect" is to add a minor 3rd (♭3) and a minor 7th (♭7) to the major pentatonic scale. Play these altered scales and listen to the tonal colors change as you hit the two altered notes.

C Major Pentatonic Scale with Added ♭3 and ♭7

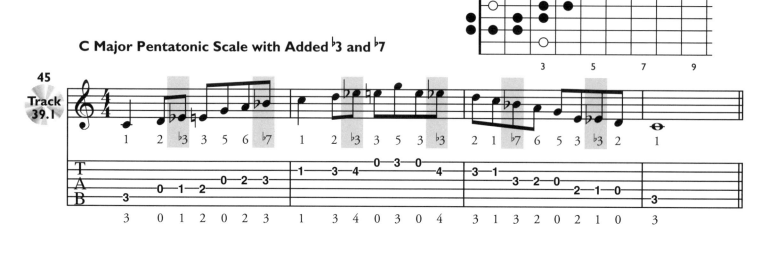

G Major Pentatonic Scale with Added ♭3 and ♭7

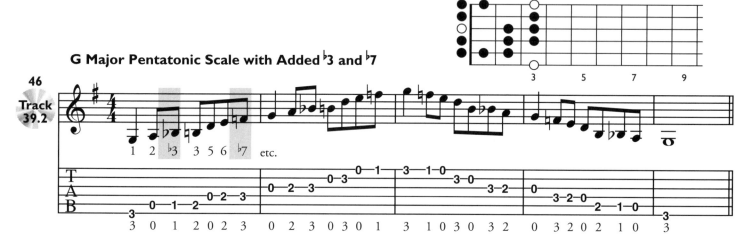

If made into a closed fingering, either of the above scales can be *transposed* or moved to other starting notes. Below is a fingering that has been transposed from the above G Major Pentatonic scale with added ♭3 and ♭7. (If you transpose the C fingering above on your own, watch out for an out of position pinky stretch on the 2nd string.)

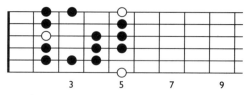

A Major Pentatonic Scale (Closed Fingering) with Added ♭3 and ♭7

♭3rd and ♭7th Fills

The major pentatonic scale with the added ♭3 and ♭7 is used (along with the unaltered major pentatonic) in bluegrass, country and folk music to fill in space between vocal phrases or to end a chord progression. Here are some popular fills played by Lester Flatt, Doc Watson and countless other country flatpickers.

Taking the Lead

You can play a major pentatonic riff (with or without the added ♭3 and ♭7) starting from the root note of any major or dominant 7th chord. Since most bluegrass and country tunes focus on the I, IV and V chords (all chords with a major quality), we can construct an entire instrumental *break* (guitar solo) using the riffs we learned on page 59.

Try the short solo below in the key of G. Watch out for the closed D Major Pentatonic scale fingering that is used to play a riff off the D (V) chord. After you have the fingerings down, you can play this solo along with the CD track. On the CD, you will hear a backing track (the chords played in an alternating bass style) and the first time through, you will hear the solo below. The second time through, you will hear only the chords, at which point you can play the solo exactly as written, or improvise your own solo using the riffs from page 59 and the scales on pages 56 and 58.

A Break for Lester

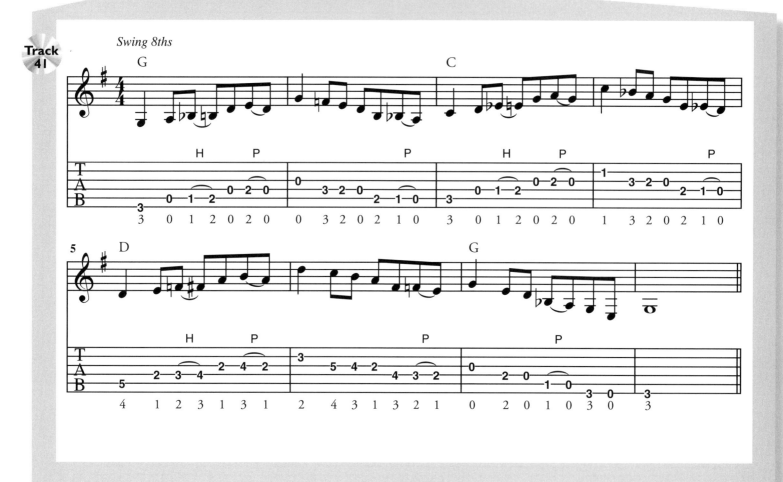

The Capo

The capo, remember, is a device that clamps onto your guitar neck at any fret to perform the function of the guitar's nut (see page 52). Bluegrass, country and folk guitar players use the capo often because the use of open strings is essential to rhythm parts and instrumental breaks. The open fingerings you've learned for the key of G, D and C are often transposed (shifted) to the keys of A, E and D (respectively) by placing a capo at the 2nd fret. Place your capo at the 2nd fret and try playing "A Break for Lester" in the key of A.

Chapter 8: Acoustic Blues

Blues music has influenced almost all other genres of American music. Bluegrass, country, folk and rock music have all been affected by blues sounds. Early travelling blues players from the Mississippi Delta, like Robert Johnson and Charlie Patton, introduced thumping acoustic rhythms and haunting melodies to the world of music. Their acoustic guitar riffs and chord changes were later carried to northern cities by blues players like Robert Nighthawk, Muddy Waters, John Lee Hooker and Howlin'

Wolf, who added electricity to the acoustic form. These sounds influenced all who were exposed to them. Bill Monroe, founder of bluegrass music, combined blues concepts with the Appalachian fiddle tune tradition. British and American rock musicians like Eric Clapton, the Rolling Stones, Fleetwood Mac and Aerosmith found themselves jamming on familiar blues changes, which became the foundation of their music.

Lesson 1: The 12-Bar Blues Progression

The most common progression used in blues music is the *12-bar blues progression*. (*Bar* is another word for measure.) This progression uses the I, IV and V chords in a specific arrangement with a few typical variations. Because this progression has been used in lots of rock and country songs, it may sound familiar and predictable to you, even if you haven't heard a lot of blues tunes. Check out the charts to the right for the order of chords in a standard 12-bar blues progression, and then a common variation on this standard *form* (structure).

Standard 12-Bar Blues		Common Variation	
Chord	Number of bars the chord is played	Chord	Number of bars the chord is played
I	4	I	1
IV	2	IV	1
I	2	I	2
V	1	IV	2
IV	1	I	2
I	2	V	1
		IV	1
		I	1
		V	1

The Dominant 7th Chord

In blues progressions, the I, IV and V chords are played as dominant 7th chords. The constant tension created by the 7th chord contributes to the blues sound. We treat these chords like the three primary chords in a key, even though technically there's only one dominant 7th chord in a key (the V7). For example, below are movable barre chords for a I–IV–V blues progression in the key of C.

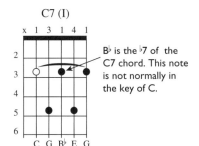

C7 (I)

B♭ is the ♭7 of the C7 chord. This note is not normally in the key of C.

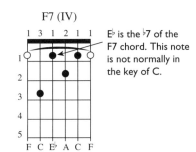

F7 (IV)

E♭ is the ♭7 of the F7 chord. This note is not normally in the key of C.

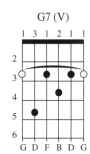

G7 (V)

The Right Hand

Blues music has undoubtedly been played on the guitar with every right-hand technique imaginable, but acoustic blues players tend to lean toward playing with their fingers over using the pick. This allows the thumb to keep a constant thumping beat on the bass strings, while leaving the fingers free to strum or pick chords and riffs. There is not a single approach to blues fingerstyle. Each player develops a style that works best for his/her rhythms and riffs. The examples in this chapter can all be played with your thumb *(p)*, index *(i)* and middle *(m)* fingers. Feel free to try different fingerings than those suggested here; some examples are even possible to play with a pick.

The Palm Mute

The *palm mute* (P.M.) is a right-hand technique used to slightly muffle the sustain or "ringing out" of notes. It is achieved by resting the heel of your right hand (the fleshy part opposite your thumb) lightly on the strings barely beyond the bridge (see page 6). You'll know when you find the right spot when you strike palm-muted strings and hear warm, deep sounding notes. Likewise, you'll know that you moved too far toward the sound hole when the pitch of the notes disappears and is replaced by a more percussive sound.

The palm mute.

Thumping Bass

Acoustic blues players add the palm mute technique to a constant *thumping bass* played by the thumb. This separates the sound of the bass from the chords and riffs and creates a two-part texture. The warm-up below will help you get used to the palm muted thumping bass. Before you start, rest the heel of your right hand on the 6th, 5th and 4th strings as described above. Now, play these bass notes with a constant downstroke of your thumb.

P.M. = Palm Mute

Thumping Bass Warm-Up

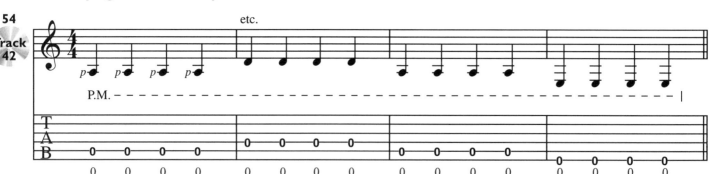

Now try a 12-bar blues progression in the key of A (using the common variation outlined on page 61). To palm mute the bass chords, again, rest the heel of your hand on the 6th, 5th and 4th strings. Let the top strings ring normally as you move your index (*i*) finger in upward sweeping motions (indicated by) to strum all three notes on the high strings at once. This tune is played with swing eighths and in this rhythm the eighth-note chords against the thumping bass can be tricky to play. Be sure to listen to the CD to get the correct rhythm.

i = Move your index finger in an upward sweeping motion to strum the notes all at once.

12-Bar Blues in A

Lesson 2: The Blues Bass

Another recognizable feature of blues is the *boogie bass* line, which originates from a blues piano style called *boogie woogie*. In this style, a piano player uses the left hand to play a repeating pattern of eighth notes against the I–IV–V blues *changes* (this term refers to the "chord changes"). The pattern uses the major pentatonic scale with the added ♭3 and ♭7 (see page 58) starting from the root note of each chord in the progression. Almost all acoustic blues guitarists adopt this style at times, sometimes playing it in

the 1st (or 2nd) position using open strings, and at other times in higher positions using movable fingerings.

Try the boogie bass line below in the key of E. Watch out for the position shifts off the V chord (measure 9). This is in the style of Leadbelly's "Bourgeois Blues."

Note that the chord symbols above the staff represent the chords implied by the boogie bass lines.

Boogie Bass in E

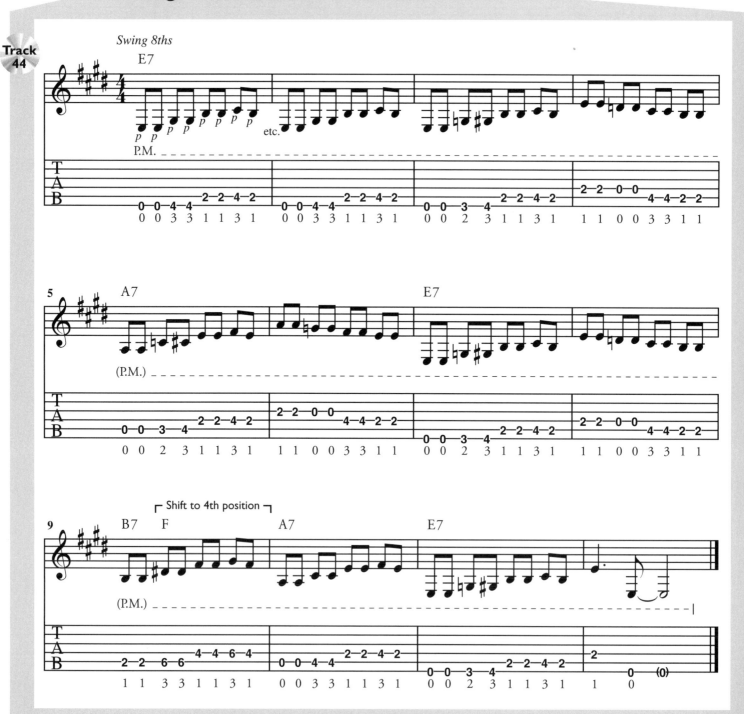

Lesson 3: The 5-6-♭7 Riff

Similar to boogie bass, the 5–6–♭7 riff starts from each root note of the I–IV–V blues progression. The difference is that in this riff, the root notes of each chord are played steadily under the moving 5–6–♭7 scale degrees above. The next example is in the style of Jimmy Page's opening acoustic guitar part to "Bring It on Home." It is in the key of E and uses the open E and A strings for the riffs off the I and IV chords respectively. Watch out for the pinky stretch off the closed V chord in measure 9. Try this one with the palm-muting technique.

Like "Boogie Bass in E" (page 64), the chord symbols above the staff represent the chords implied by the 5–6–♭7 riff.

5-6-♭7 Blues in E

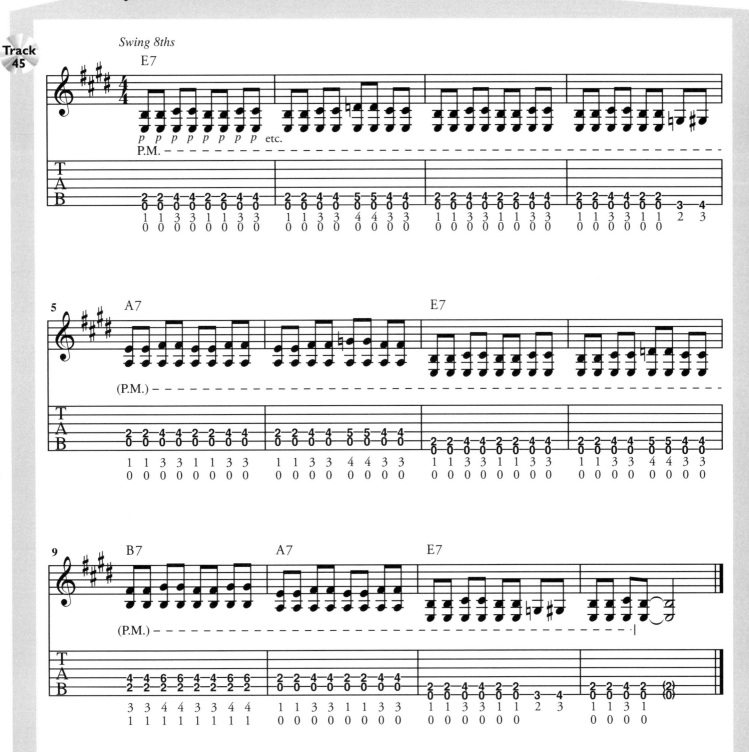

Lesson 4: The Minor Pentatonic Scale

In traditional acoustic blues songs, it is often hard to distinguish between what is major and what is minor. In fact, a five-note minor-type scale called the *minor pentatonic scale,* can be used to create riffs and melodies that fit over the I–IV–V blues progression (which is considered to be in a major key). The minor pentatonic scale uses scale degrees 1–♭3–4–5–♭7 of the major scale.

The altered notes that are introduced (the ♭3 and ♭7) work because they are the same notes that we find in the dominant 7th versions of our I and IV chords used in blues progressions. For example, in the key of C, the ♭3 is an E♭ and the ♭7 is a B♭. B♭ the ♭7 of C (the I chord) and E♭ is the ♭7 of F (the IV chord).

The C Minor Pentatonic Scale

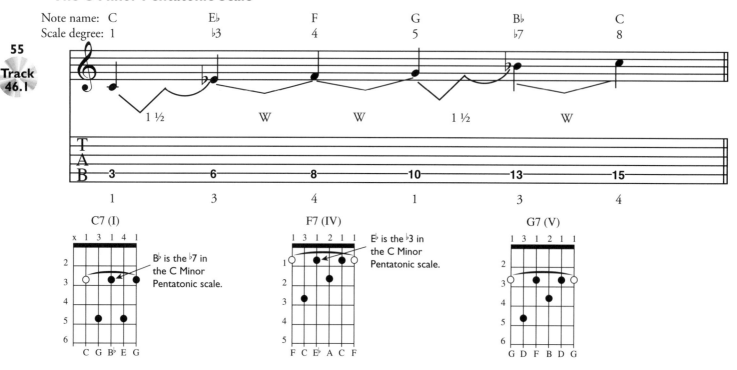

Here are some usable fingerings for the minor pentatonic scale. The first is an E Minor Pentatonic scale in the 1st position using open strings. (If you compare this fingering to the G Major Pentatonic scale on page 56, you'll find that these two scales have the same notes, but different tonics. This makes them relative major and minor scales as described on page 35.)

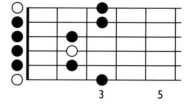

E Minor Pentatonic Scale (Open Fingering)

This closed fingering starts from the note A and follows the same contour as the E Minor Pentatonic scale on page 66.

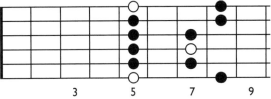

A Minor Pentatonic Scale (Closed Fingering)

57
Track 47.1

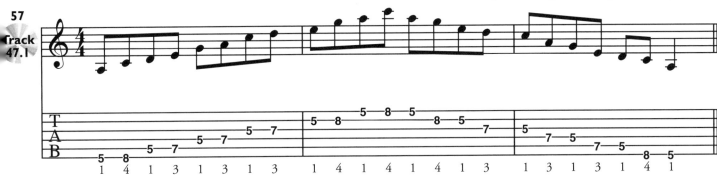

Now, here's an open fingering for the A Minor Pentatonic scale. This one starts from the 5th string.

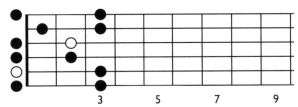

A Minor Pentatonic Scale (Open Fingering)

58
Track 47.2

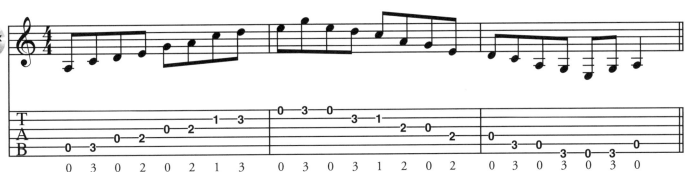

Finally, here's a closed E Minor Pentatonic scale in the 7th position. It starts from the 5th string and follows the same contour as the above A Minor Pentatonic scale.

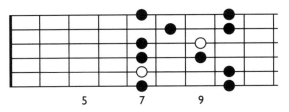

E Minor Pentatonic Scale (Closed Fingering)

59
Track 47.3

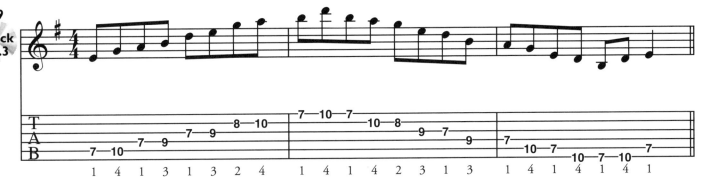

Lesson 5: Blues Riffs, Intros and Turnarounds

Blues players often combine the palm-muted thumping bass, the boogie bass and the 5–6–♭7 in the same 12-bar blues progression. This is enough to carry the tune, but players use other riffs to make things even more interesting.

Almost all blues tunes start with some sort of riff that kicks off the song. This *intro* (introduction) occurs before the first measure of the progression and leads to a V chord. Often, the intro riff is the same riff that is played at the

very last measure (or two) of the progression. Played at the end, the riff is called a *turnaround* as it takes us to the V chord and sets us up to start the progression again or end the tune.

Below are some ideas that can be used for intros and/or turnarounds.

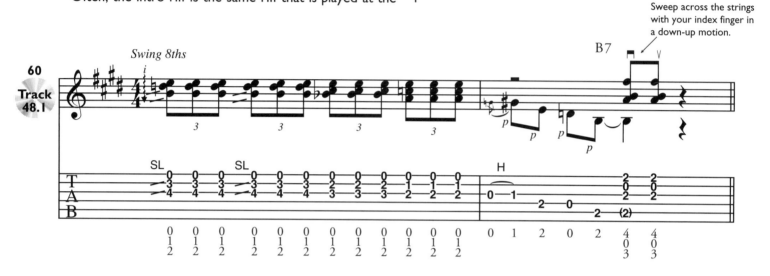

This riff works well using your *m* and *i* fingers. It can also be played with the pick.

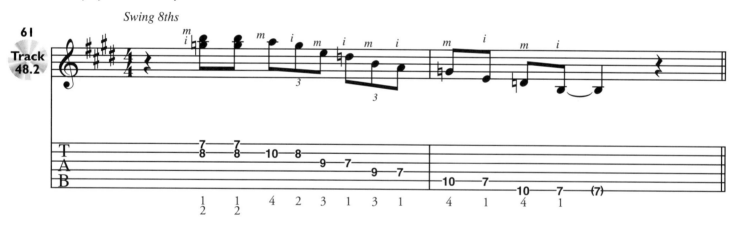

Try this one just using your thumb.

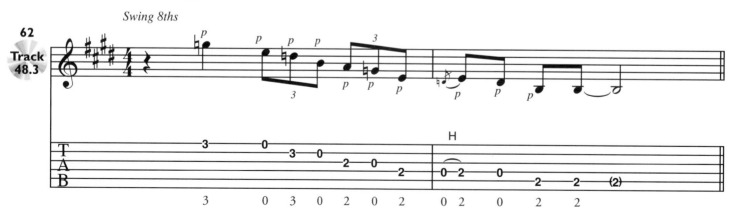

Here's a two-part intro/turnaround that combines the thumping bass with a riff on the upper strings.

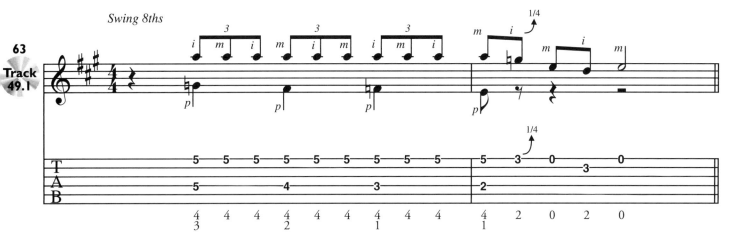

Try this single-string riff with your pick.

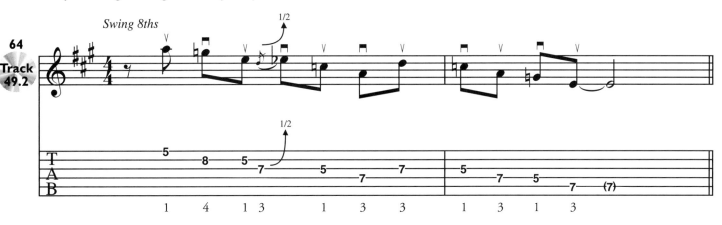

This turnaround works well when played entirely with the upward sweeping motion of your index finger.

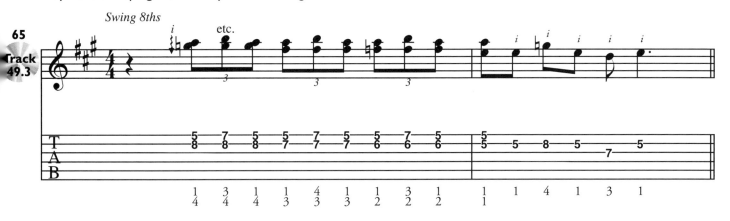

Note: Another component of blues music is the use of *call and response*. This tradition is rooted in early gospel music and the songs of field and railroad workers. Traditionally, a single "caller" sings a line, which is answered by a "chorus" responding with the same line. A similar effect occurs in blues music today when an instrument such as the guitar fills in the space between vocal lines with riffs that seem to respond to the vocal phrase.

Lesson 6: The ♭5 and the ♮3

Blues players often add two more notes to their minor pentatonic riffs. One common note used in passing is the ♭5. Adding a ♭5 to the minor pentatonic scale creates the distinct, tense sound of the *blues scale,* which consists of scale degrees 1–♭3–4–♭5–5–♭7. The other added note has the opposite effect. Inserting the ♮3 (the unaltered 3rd from the key) when the progression is on the I chord creates a feeling of resolution and reminds us that we are in a major key.

Playing the Blues Scale

You don't need to learn new fingerings to play the blues scale. Instead, just simply add the note that is between the 4th and 5th of the scale. This added note, the ♭5 (lowered 5th), can also be thought of as a ♯4 (raised 4th). These two scale degrees are enharmonic equivalents (see page 8). Traditionally, when a melody or scale is ascending, sharps are used to alter notes; when descending, flats are used.

This is why the same pitch is written as a ♯4 (A♯) and a ♭5 (B♭) in the following example.

The E Blues Scale

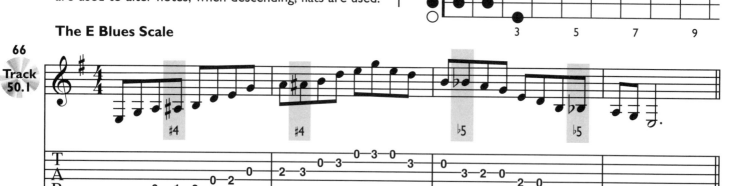

Adding the ♮3

When we add the ♮3 to a minor pentatonic riff we are not forming a new scale. We are just resolving the ♭3 (an altered note that is part of the minor pentatonic scale) to the ♮3 (a scale degree belonging to the key of the progression). The ♮3 sounds best when it is played over the I chord, and it is often preceded by the ♭3 for contrast. Try these minor pentatonic riffs with ♮3 resolutions. These types of riffs also work well as endings to blues songs.

Here's a solo (in this case, "solo" means a piece in which you play the melody and harmony at the same time) that combines all the concepts of this chapter. The suggested right-hand fingering indications will help you get the acoustic blues feel. Wherever there are three simultaneous notes to play, your index (i) finger sweeps across the strings in the familiar upward attack. The 6th, 5th and 4th strings can all be palm muted. It may take some time to get comfortable with this piece, but be patient—and listen to some Lightnin' Hopkins, Robert Johnson and Charlie Patton along the way.

Don't Cha Wanna Go

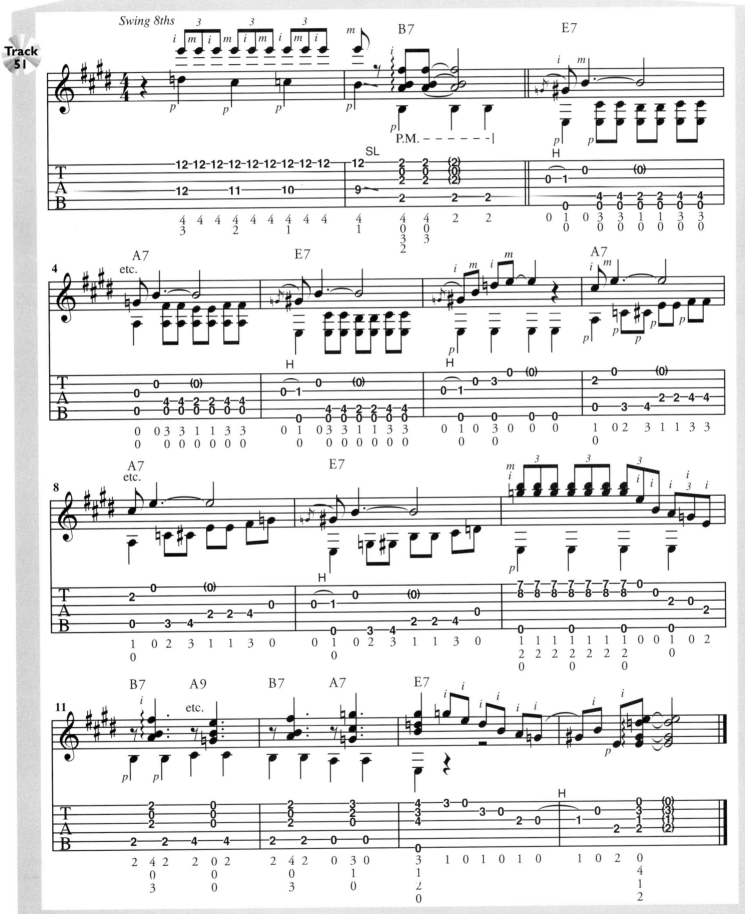

Chapter 9: Acoustic Guitar in Rock

The acoustic guitar has always been important in rock music. Countless rock bands have made use of the distinct texture of the acoustic guitar to contrast against their driving, electrified sound. Even the crunchiest, hardest, most ultra-modern rock bands, like System of a Down or Staind, use the acoustic guitar to introduce a song. Due to the popularity of the "unplugged" phenomenon over the last 10 to 15 years, alternative rock pioneers like Nirvana and Alice in Chains reworked or wrote material to play in acoustic settings. Today, there are artists that have built new brands of rock music around the acoustic guitar. Players like Ben Harper and Jack Johnson, drawing on traditional roots, remind us of the simple beauty of the acoustic guitar, while others like Dave Matthews and Ani DiFranco redefine the instrument (and rock for that matter) with new chord fingerings and percussive textures.

Lesson 1: The Power Chord

The *power chord* is an essential feature of rock music. Guitarists affectionately call this two-note fingering a "chord" and use it as such, but in fact it is just an interval of a perfect 5th. The power chord positions the root on a lower string and the 5th on an adjacent string above it. It is missing the 3rd and therefore can be used in place of either a major or minor chord (since the 3rd is what determines the major or minor quality of a chord). Also, these chords appear as three-string chords when their roots are doubled by an octave.

Try the power chord voicings below. Remember, closed fingerings are moveable and can be moved to any root note. Notice the chord symbols. The letter name tells you the root of the power chord and the 5 indicates that it is an interval of a perfect 5th.

Power Chord Voicings

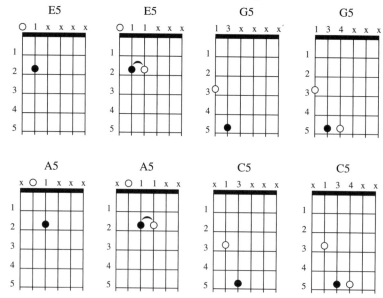

Power Chord Palm Mutes

Rock guitarists often use the palm mute when playing power chords. To keep a steady, even sound, play consecutive palm-muted eighth notes with downstrokes of the pick.

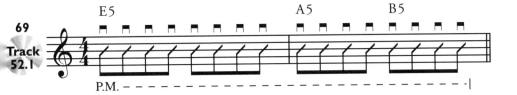

Accenting Beats 2 and 4

One defining characteristic of rock music in $\frac{4}{4}$ time is the strong accent on beats 2 and 4 (called the *backbeat*). This is usually where the drummer hits the snare drum. Palm muting makes it easy to accent this beat with the drummer by simply lifting the heel of your right hand off the strings on beats 2 and 4. Don't lift too far off the strings, as you'll want to get right back to the palm mute on the offbeats. Try it.

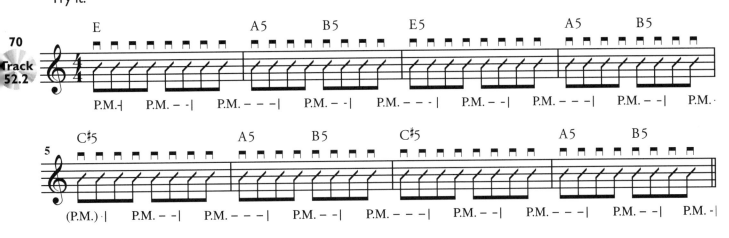

Another way to accent beats 2 and 4 is by totally muting the strings as you strike them with the pick. This technique is explained at the top of page 74.

Rhythm Builder: The Mute Stroke

The guitar is a percussive instrument, especially the acoustic guitar. You can add more texture and rhythm to a tune by bringing out this quality with the *mute stroke*, which totally mutes the strings as you strum. There are two ways to perform a mute stroke. Practice these steps to get the feel for this technique. Mute strokes are indicated with the symbol ×.

The Right-Hand Mute

1. Rest the heel of your right hand close to the sound hole. (See Step 1 photo.)

2. While resting on the strings, move your pick across the strings in a downward strum-like motion. (This is like a palm mute moved too far away from the bridge.) (See Step 2 photo.)

3. Now, with your hand off the strings in a strum-ready position, try to strum and rest your heel in one motion. If you do this right you'll hear a sharp, raspy, percussive sound like a snare drum. (See Step 3 photo.)

Step 1

Step 2

Step 3

The Left-Hand Mute

When there are no open strings involved in a chord voicing, it can be muted by releasing the pressure of your left-hand fingers, while keeping contact with the strings. Your right hand strums the chord as it normally would. You can utilize this approach with closed fingerings whenever you wish to use a mute stroke.

This tune is in the style of Kurt Cobain's early acoustic guitar playing. It incorporates power chords, barre chords, palm mutes and the mute stroke. Don't be alarmed by the open-string figures on the offbeats. They will occur naturally when lifting your fingers to change chords while maintaining your constant down-up right-hand motion.

Anyone Want a Cracker?

× = Mute stroke

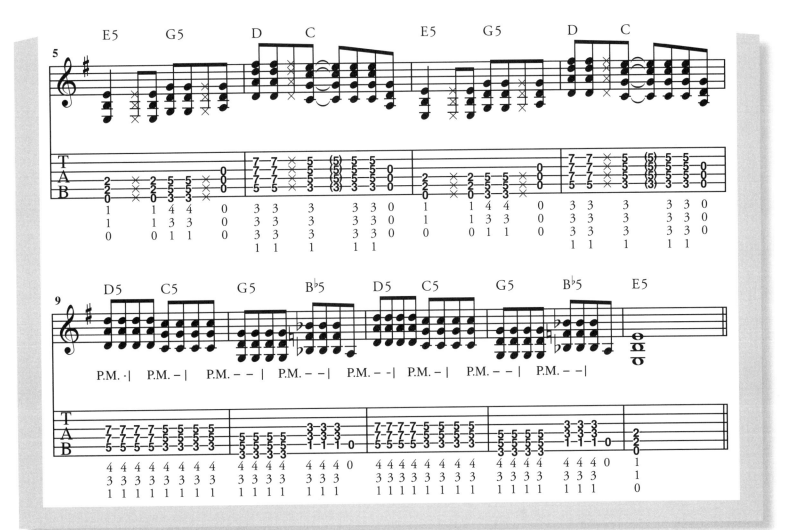

Lesson 2: Drone Strings

Rock guitarists often keep open strings ringing while strumming progressions of power chords or major and minor chords. Notes that stay the same as others are changing are called *pedal tones* or *drone notes*. Constant droning strings, played against chord changes, produce a big, open sound that ties all the chords together.

"Drone and Alone" is a progression that uses an E5, C5 and D5 on the inner strings, with constant drone notes on the outer strings. It uses the classic syncopated strum learned on page 20.

Drone and Alone

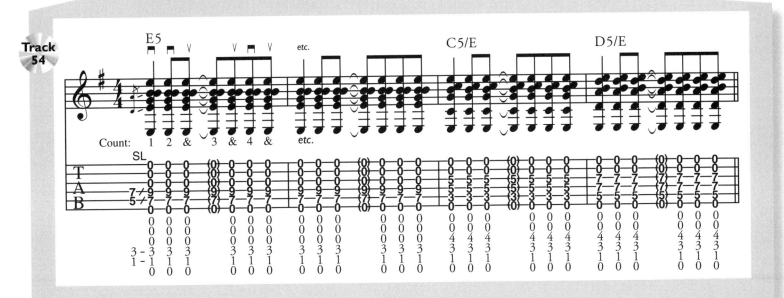

Lesson 3: Suspended Chords

A good way to add some tension to a basic chord progression is by using *suspended* or *sus* chords. These chords replace the 3rd of a triad with the 2nd or 4th scale degree. The 2nd or 4th produces an unresolved sound that resolves nicely to the 3rd, but often in rock tunes this chord is left unresolved to leave the listener wanting more. Like the power chord, a suspended chord does not have a 3rd and can be used in place of either a major or minor chord.

Making Major and Minor Chords Suspended

Any major chord can be transformed into a suspended chord by moving the 3rd down a whole step to form a *sus2* (suspended 2nd) chord, or moving it up one half step to form a *sus4* (suspended 4th) chord. Any minor chord can be turned into a sus chord by lowering the 3rd one half step to form a sus2, or raising it a whole step to form a sus4. Below are some common suspended chord fingerings from different root notes. The diagrams show sus4 chords moving to sus2, then resolving to the unaltered triad. The scale degrees are written underneath each chord diagram (R=Root, 3=3rd, 5=5th, 2=2nd, and 4=4th). Notice that the sus chord fingerings are the same whether the chord resolves to a major or a minor chord.

Open Suspended Chords

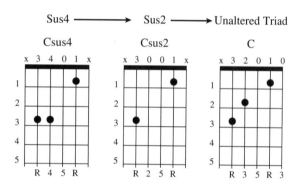

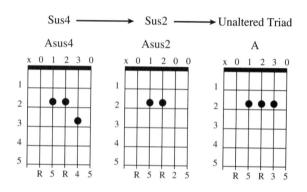

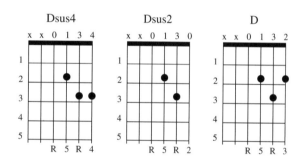

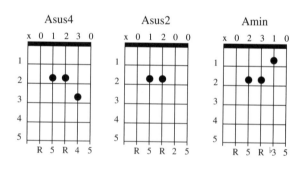

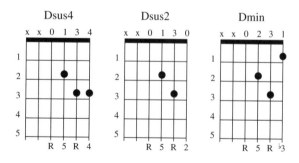

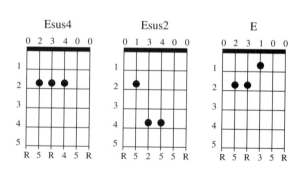

Movable Suspended Chords

Below are some useful fingerings of movable suspended chords. These voicings will allow you to play suspended chords anywhere on the neck, by placing the fingering at the desired root note. These fingerings open up a lot of possibilities, but they are a challenge to form. Be patient when working on these; you'll get them in no time.

Movable Suspended Chords (Roots on the 6th String)

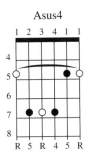

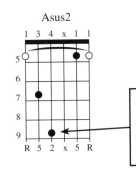

This is a big stretch for your pinky. Besides stretching a great distance, your pinky must slightly touch the 3rd string to keep it from ringing in the barre.

Movable Suspended Chords (Roots on the 5th String)

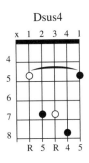

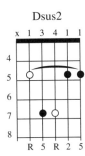

Here's a rock ballad based on Staind's "Everything Changes." It's in $\frac{3}{4}$ time and uses sus chords and drone strings. Watch your picking motion, as dotted eighth notes are used in this rhythm.

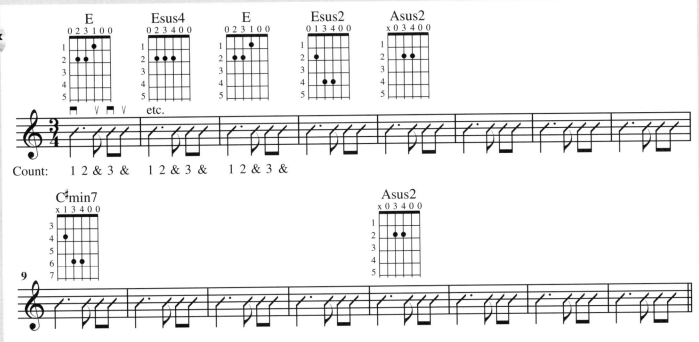

Not Every String Changes

Rhythm Builder: Syncopated Strumming with Sixteenth Notes

It's time to learn a syncopated sixteenth-note strumming pattern used in many tunes. Like the syncopated strum using eighth notes (see page 20), this rhythm uses ties to shift emphases from the onbeats to the weaker parts of the beat. Let's build this one in steps as well.

1. First, take a look at the entire pattern and compare the picking motions to a measure of all sixteenth notes. The *dotted eighth note* on beat 2 is held for a duration of three sixteenth notes. Downstrokes and upstrokes in parentheses (⊓) (∨) indicate where the pick passes over the strings without striking the strings.

A dotted eighth note rings for the duration of three sixteenth notes or an eighth note tied to a sixteenth.

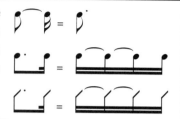

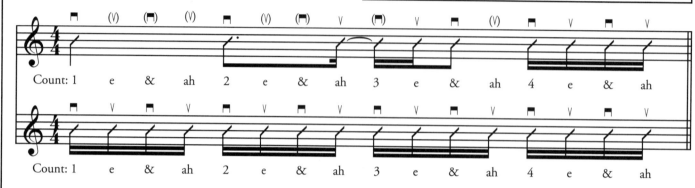

2. Now, let's focus on the first two beats. Remember to keep a constant down-up picking motion as you play this, even on beats 3 and 4 where no strings are actually being strummed.

71
Track
56.1

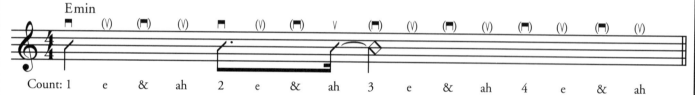

3. Now, add beat 3 and put a quarter note on beat 4.

72
Track
56.2

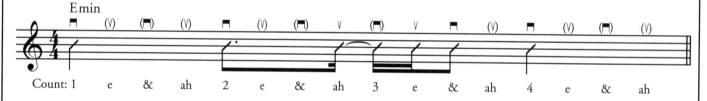

4. Step 3 produces the overall feel of this sixteenth-note syncopated strum. Beat 4 is left for subtle variations from one measure to the next. Check out a few variations below.

73
Track
56.3

74
Track
56.4

75
Track
56.5

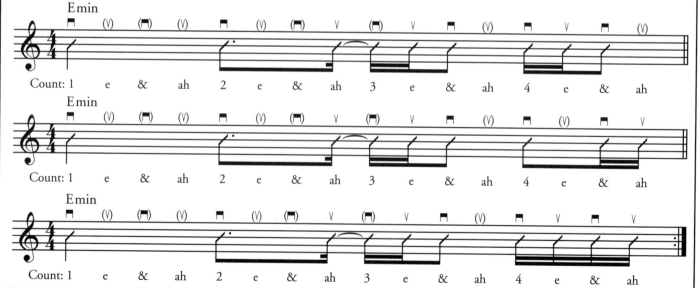

"The Interstellar Pilot" is based on the changes to Stone Temple Pilots' "Interstate Love Song." It uses the syncopated sixteenth-note strumming pattern. The movable major and minor forms here are played without barres to create droning open strings. You will need a barre at measure 4 to grab the G#sus4 chord and its resolution to G# Major.

The Interstellar Pilot

Track 57.1

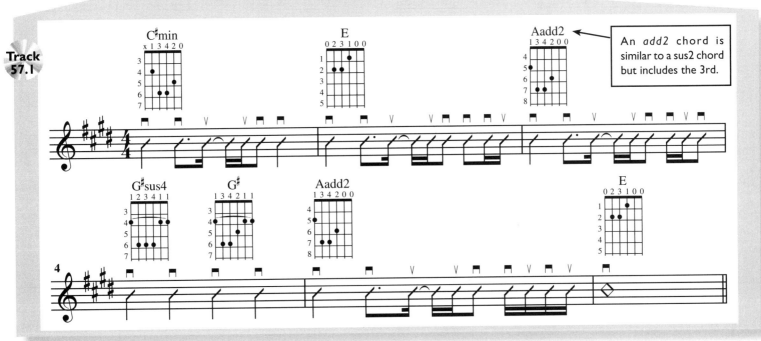

An *add2* chord is similar to a sus2 chord but includes the 3rd.

Here's a chord progression in the style of Dave Matthews' "Crash into Me." An an independent bass line is produced by using the bass-strum technique and lots of drone strings are used.

Syncopated Bass-Strum

Track 57.2

The tune below is in the style of Jack Johnson's "Sitting, Waiting, Wishing," which uses the mute stroke in a similar way. Since this song uses movable 7th chords, the mutes are accomplished by slightly lifting the pressure of your left hand off the strings as you strum. Also, notice that your pick separates the low notes of the chord from the high notes. Splitting the strum into two parts like this can make a piece of music more rhythmically interesting. This tune, with the mute strokes on beats 2 and 4, has the sound of a bassist, guitarist and drummer playing together.

Sittin', Strummin', Mutin'

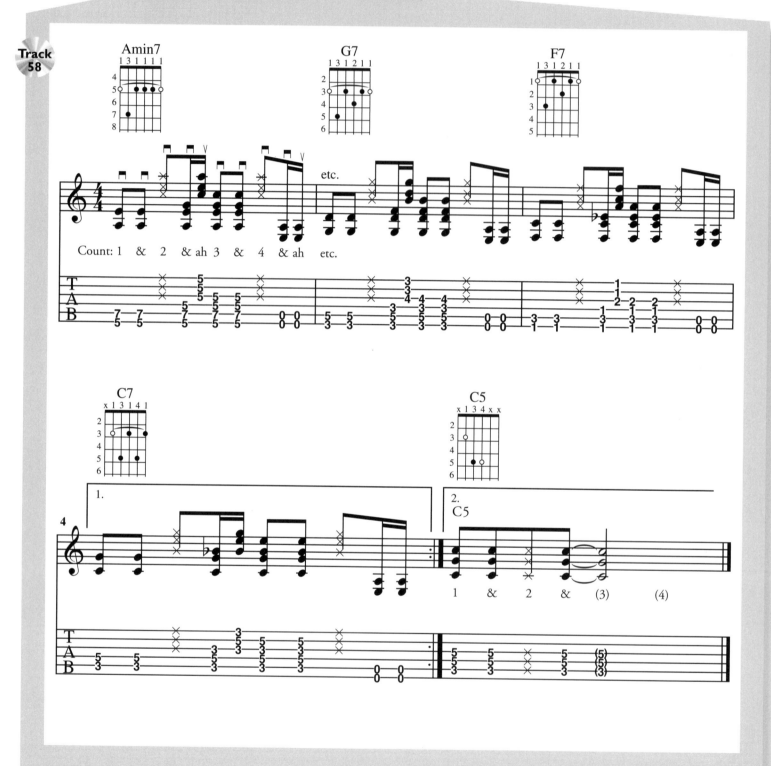

Lesson 4: Pick Arpeggios

Along with big-sounding strumming rhythms that use drone strings and suspended chords, rock guitarists also use the pick to play arpeggios across chord forms (similar to the fingerstyle arpeggios introduced in Chapter 6, page 48).

"Goodbye, Country" is in the style of Green Day's "Good Riddance." The arpeggio pattern in this tune uses the same rhythm and picking motion as the eighth-note syncopated strum from page 20. As the tune progresses, the arpeggio gives way to the "split-strum" feel we encountered on page 80.

Goodbye, Country

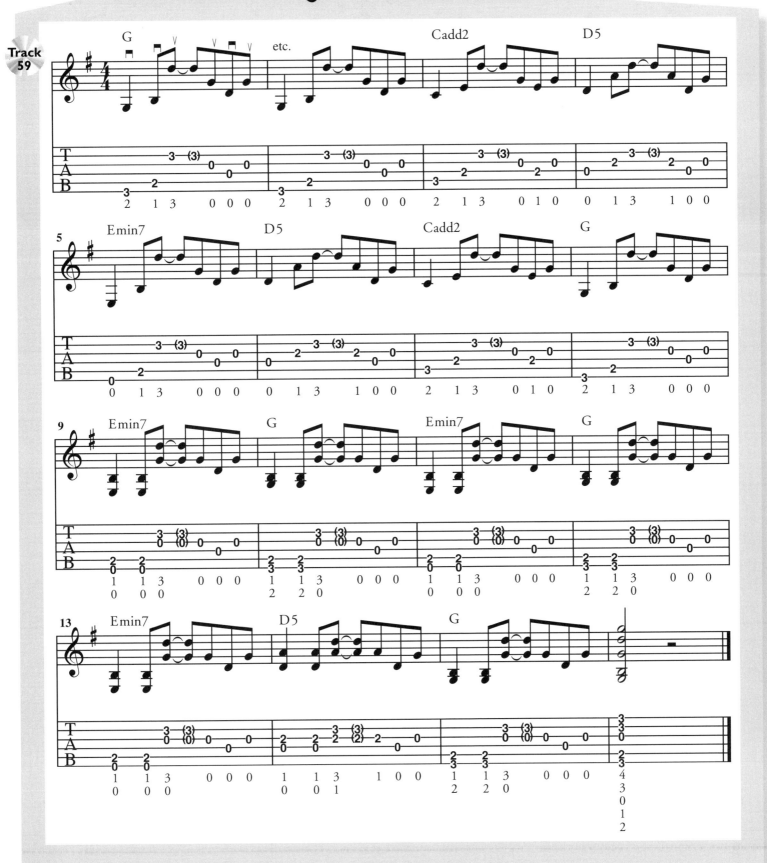

"Pick Your Friends" is a progression that embellishes arpeggiated chords with slurs. It's in the style of "My Friends," by The Red Hot Chili Peppers, which spices up acoustic arpeggios with similar riffs.

Pick Your Friends

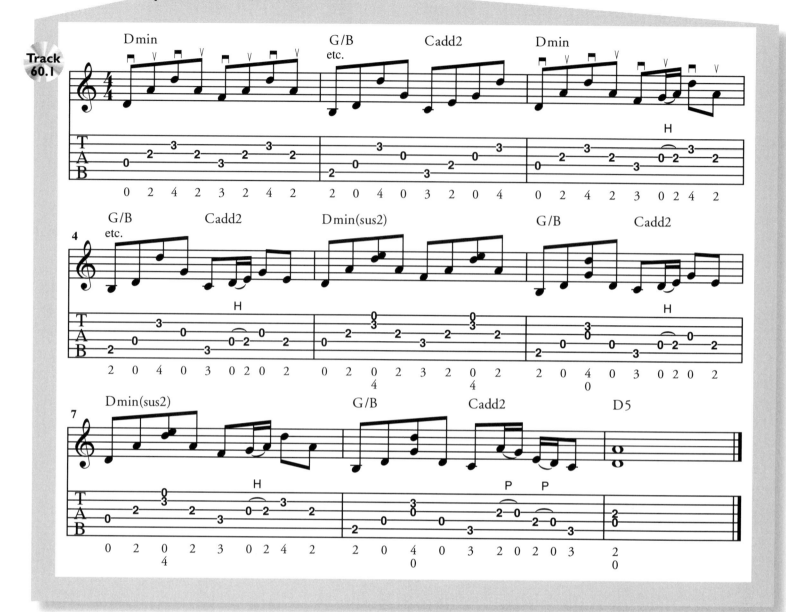

This next one is in the style of the Rolling Stones' "Angie." It features the sixteenth-note rhythm we learned on page 78, with separated bass, arpeggios, movable chords and sus chords.

Agnus

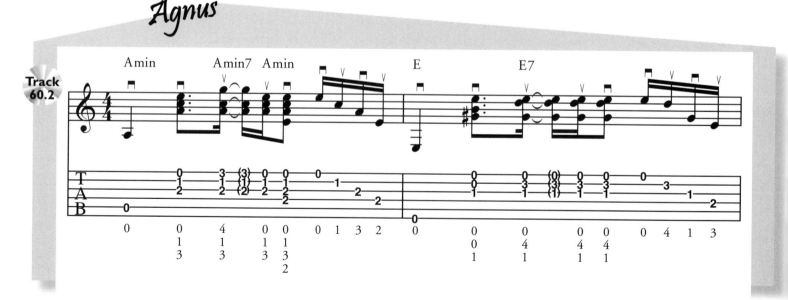

Riff Builder: Hybrid Picking

Hybrid picking is a combination of fingerstyle and flatpick technique. It allows you to simultaneously attack two non-adjacent strings, one with a downstroke of the pick and the other with a free finger of the right hand. Since you hold the pick between your thumb and index finger, your middle and ring fingers are actually free to pluck notes. With some practice, it is possible to execute intricate fingerstyle-like patterns with this hybrid technique. Most songs use the technique sparingly for necessary accents and effects.

Let's work our way into this technique:

1. First, form a C chord, and with a downstroke of the pick, attack the bass note alone.

2. Now, with your middle (*m*) finger, pluck the 2nd string. The finger should move upward toward your palm.

3. Next, coordinating the two movements, attack the bass with the pick and the 2nd string with your middle (*m*) finger simultaneously. As the pick moves down, the finger comes up. The two sounds will not be even at first. The bass will come out louder than the 2nd string until your finger gets used to the motion.

4. Now, try coordinating the same bass with your ring (*a*) finger on the 1st string. Again, it will take time for this finger to get comfortable.

To perform hybrid picking, you may alternate between both of your free fingers or choose just one of them. You'll be surprised how much extra sound is created just by an occasional double- or triple-note attack.

Here's a chord progression that uses arpeggios accented with hybrid-picking attacks on beats 1 and 3 of each measure. You can play all the eighth notes of this example with downstrokes of the pick. This will make it easier to focus on the hybrid attacks. The *rit.* above the last measure

is an abbreviation of the word *ritardando* or *ritard*. This is a musical expression that tells the performer to slow the tempo (beat). Listen to the CD track to get a sense of how this sounds.

Hybrid Bridge

Track 61

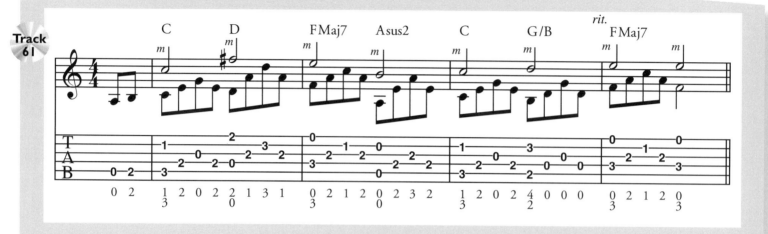

Lesson 5: Muted String Chord Fingerings

Modern acoustic guitarists find ways to bring out the percussive nature of the acoustic guitar. They often treat the guitar like a drum, using it to create a layers of rhythm in a song. As you know, the mute stroke is a useful tool that simulates drumming on the guitar, but choosing certain chord voicings over others can also contribute to the guitar's percussive sound.

Let's explore some voicings used by guitarists like Dave Matthews. These are three-note fingerings of triads or implied 7th chords. (Remember, full 7th chords are four-note chords, see page 44.) These chord fingerings skip over strings that must be muffled when the chord is strummed. Besides adding a percussive feel, these chords bring an element of jazz and funk to your acoustic guitar playing.

To the right are some 7th chord voicings with the root note on the 6th string (we can refer to chords with the root on the 6th string as *root 6* chords). For the AMaj7 and the A7, let your 1st finger rest across all six strings, while the fingertip frets the root of the chord on the 6th string. This will muffle all unwanted strings. For the Amin7, let the pad of your 2nd finger muffle the 5th string as the fingertip frets the root of the chord on the 6th string. To muffle the 1st and 2nd strings, rest your 1st finger on them.

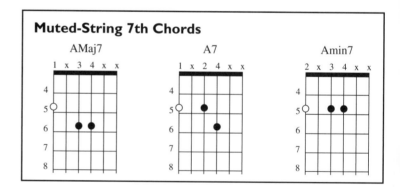

Now, try the muted-string triad voicings to the right. For the F chord, let your 1st finger do all the muffling. For the F/A, your 3rd finger must fret the 6th string and muffle the 5th string while your 1st finger frets the 4th string and muffles the 1st and 2nd. Do the same for the F/C.

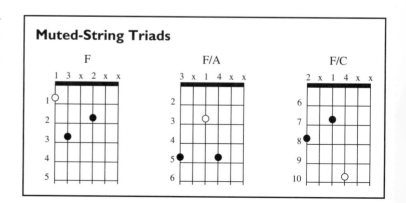

Here's a song that will get you accustomed to changing
between muted-string chord voicings.

Muted Matthews

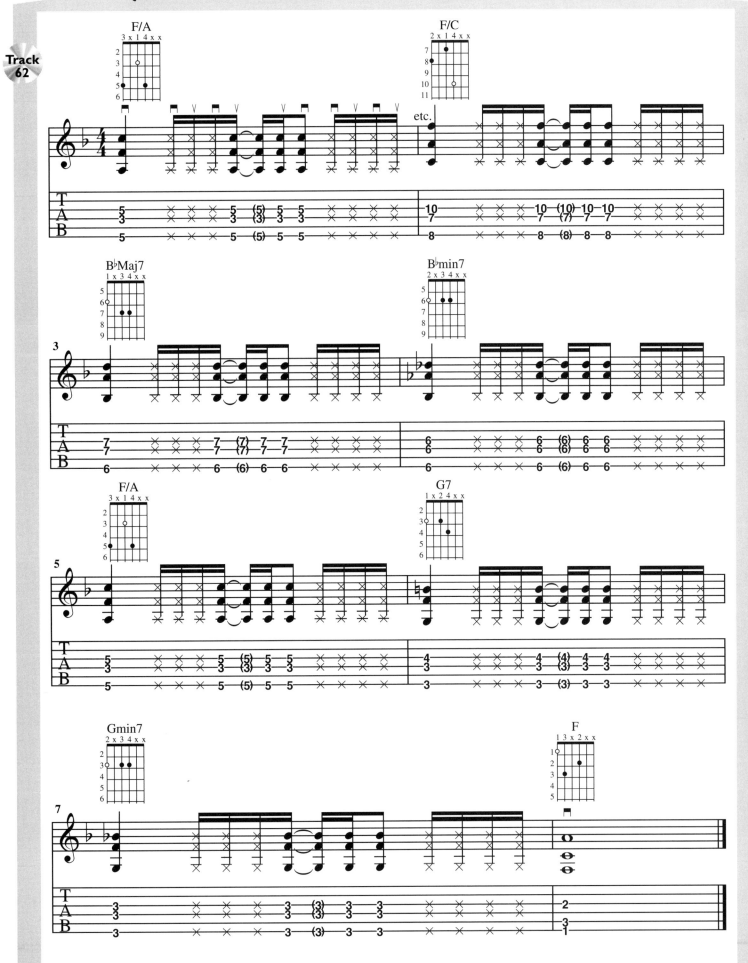

"Play What You Play" uses the mute stroke and muted-string voicings; it also changes time signature. This is typical of progressive rock music that is influenced by jazz and funk. Many Dave Matthews songs have similar time changes. This tune is in the style of Matthews' "What Would You Say?"

Play What You Play

Lesson 6: Acoustic Rock Solos

Rock music draws on the whole spectrum of genres and traditions. This is apparent when the acoustic guitar takes the lead. The bluegrass and blues concepts learned in Chapter 7 and Chapter 8 regarding the major pentatonic scale, the minor pentatonic scale and the blues scale are all used to create acoustic rock solos. These solos are connected to the blues through the use of frequent bends and a focus on blue notes such as the ♭3rd and ♭7th. Since rock guitarists apply traditional techniques to a wide range of chord changes in a variety of keys, most become good at finding fingerings for their riffs and ideas anywhere on the guitar neck.

Two New Fingerings

Before we try some solos, let's take a moment to start connecting our scale fingerings across the fretboard. Using the key of D as an example, we'll learn two new closed fingerings we can use to connect the scales we've learned.

The fingering below is in the 4th position with the tonic on the 5th string. The minus sign (-) next to a left hand fingering tells you to stretch the finger one fret lower out of position. This fingering is labeled Form 2; you'll soon see why.

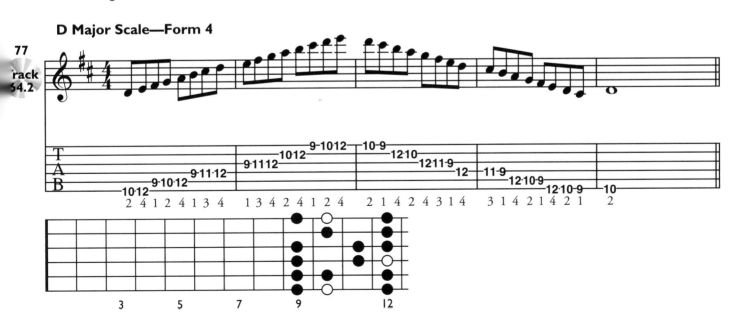

Form 4 is in the 9th position with the tonic on the 6th string.

Connecting the Major Scale Forms

On page 30, you learned a fingering for the D Major scale in the 2nd position. Let's call that fingering Form 1. On page 31 you learned a movable fingering for the A Major scale in the 2nd position. Let's use that fingering but shift it to the 9th position to make it a D Major scale as well.

We'll call this Form 3. Now we have four overlapping forms across the neck. This covers much of the fretboard, as you can see in the diagram below.

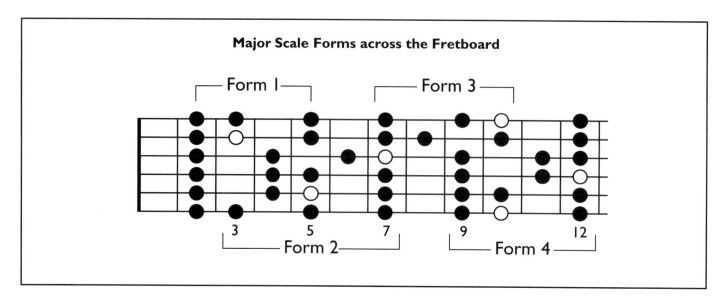

Connecting the Pentatonic Scale Forms

As you learned in Chapter 7, the major pentatonic scale is just like the major scale, except there are no 4th or 7th scale degrees. Therefore, the positions you just practiced to connect the major scale forms apply to the major pentatonic scale as well. It is helpful to note that these fingerings can all sound like their relative minor key just by starting from the 6th scale degree. Remember, if the focus on the 6th scale degree is prolonged throughout a song, then what was the 6th degree in major becomes the 1st degree in the relative minor. The diagram below lays out the pentatonic scales in the four forms we've been using. The major root and minor root are marked with different symbols.

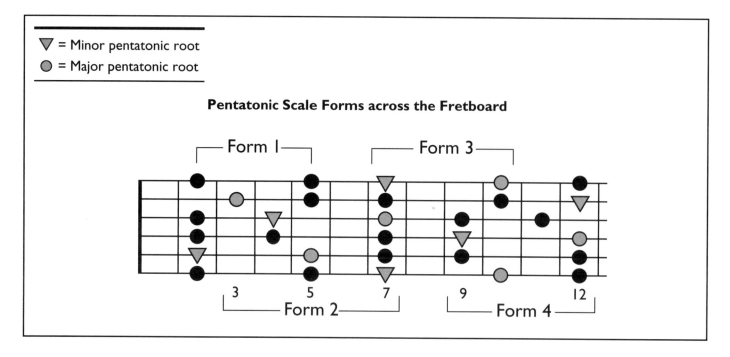

Now that you're becoming more familiar with your fretboard, let's reinforce these scale fingerings with some acoustic guitar solos in the styles of a few popular rock tunes.

"Wish I Was at Your Place" is a solo in the style of Pink Floyd's "Wish You Were Here." It makes use of all the slurs you've learned so far. By moving Form 4 of the pentatonic fingerings on page 88 to the 2nd position, we get a solo that is constructed from a G Major Pentatonic scale. Occasionally, open strings are used instead of the fretted notes. Occurring on long notes at the end of riffs, the open strings vary the texture of the notes and help them sustain.

On the CD, the lead guitar drops out after playing the solo once. The backing track continues, allowing you to play the solo as written or improvise a solo of your own.

Wish I Was at Your Place

Rhythm Builder: Sixteenth-Note Triplets

Remembering that a triplet evenly distributes three note divisions where there would normally be two, let's now consider *sixteenth-note triplets*. If two sixteenth notes take up the time of half a beat, then a sixteenth-note triplet also takes up a half a beat. This type of triplet is written as three sixteenth notes beamed together with a *3* above or below the beamed group (see example to the right).

If a beat is filled with two sixteenth-note triplets, then the beam is drawn across the entire beat. You will see the number three above the beam twice to signify two triplet groups (see example to the right).

Sixteenth-Note Triplet

= Half beat

Two Sixteenth-Note Triplets

= Full beat

These rhythms will help you hear and feel sixteenth-note triplets in a rhythmic context. Follow the picking motions as you play these examples on the open 1st string.

"Thanks to Slurs" is in the style of Jimmy Page's solo on the Led Zeppelin tune "Thank You." This solo moves across the fretboard using Forms 1, 2 and 3 of the D Major scale, with an occasional pentatonic run. Notice the added ♭3 in the fifth measure, which creates a bluesy effect. Watch for the sixteenth-note triplets; in measure 7, they are executed with hammer-on slurs (just the first note of each triplet is attacked while the other two are slurred). Carefully executed slurs, such as these, make it easier to play fast passages of notes.

On the CD, the solo is played once. The backing track continues, allowing you to play the solo as written or improvise your own using the scale forms on page 88.

Remember, a minus sign (-) next to a left-hand fingering means to stretch the finger one fret out of position. Just stretch your finger, don't move your hand.

Thanks to Slurs

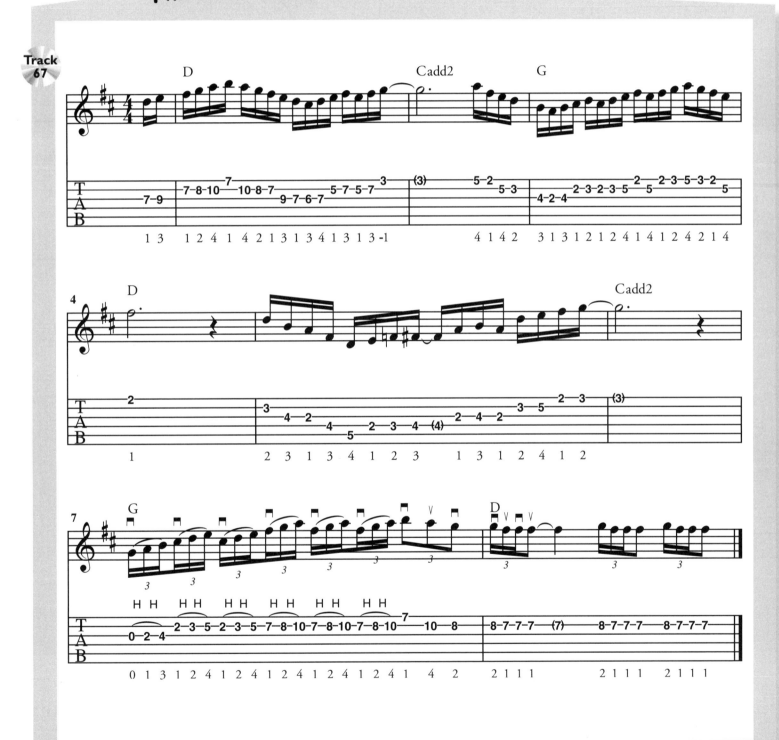

Chapter 10: The Song

This chapter discusses song structure and common terms used for the parts of a *song*. When you become familiar with these terms, you will be able to navigate through songbooks as well as construct your own songs based on these concepts. In modern times, we use the word "song" loosely to refer to any tune that we listen to, but strictly speaking, a piece of music is a song if it has lyrics sung by a vocalist. Most of the music we've covered so far has been meant to accompany a vocalist. Now, we'll explore the parts of a song and reference some songwriting techniques used by pivotal guitarist-songwriters like Bob Dylan, James Taylor, Jim Croce and Paul Simon. Their approach has influenced new generations of guitar playing songwriters like Tracy Chapman, Sheryl Crow, Jewel, Jeff Buckley, Jack Johnson and many more.

Lesson 1: Phrasing

The basic building block of music is the musical *phrase*. A phrase is a group of smoothly connected notes that convey a musical idea. Similar to lines in poems or sentences in novels, musical phrases are grouped together to construct larger sections of a piece (like the stanza of a poem). As we'll see in the next lesson, there are some common labels given to the sections of a song.

"Phrasing the Section" demonstrates a group of four phrases that are supported by a progression of three repeating chords. A passage like this could be a complete section of a song. Note the long curved lines above notes. These are not slurs or ties; they are *phrase markers* and are meant to indicate a connected idea or phrase. Phrases aren't always marked in a songbook. Usually, a player must interpret the music himself/herself to outline phrases. The phrases below are made from Form 1 of the pentatonic scale (page 88).

Phrasing the Section

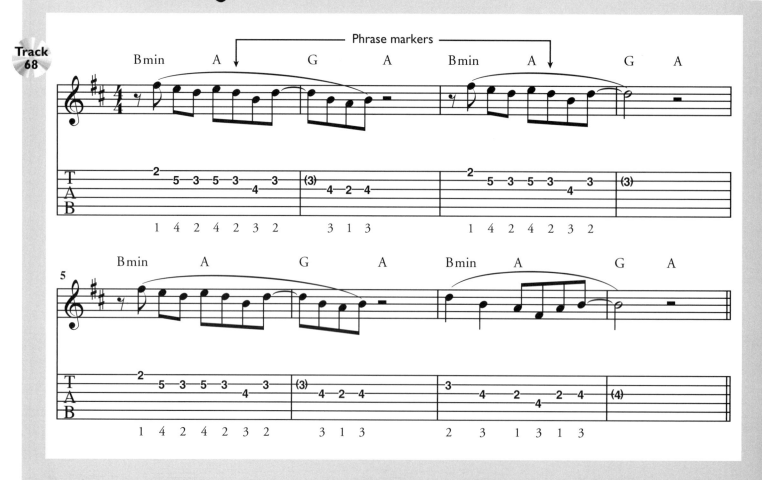

Riff Builder: Articulation and Dynamic Marks

Symbols are used to shape written music into phrases. *Articulation* symbols function in music like commas, periods and voice intonation in poetry. *Dynamic marks* tell you how loud or soft to play notes in general. You can use this page as a reference when you come across these articulation and dynamic markings in songbooks.

Staccato Mark

A dot placed above or below a note symbol is a *staccato mark*. This articulation tells you stop the note from ringing for its full duration. Staccato marks make notes sound separate from each other, which is the opposite of the smooth, connected sound created by slurs (called *legato*). You can make a note sound staccato by slightly lifting your left-hand pressure after you attack the note, or you can place a right-hand finger (or the pick) on the string to stop it from ringing.

Accent Mark

A symbol above or below a note that resembles an open triangle turned on its side is an *accent mark*. It tells you to emphasize the note by attacking it slightly harder than unmarked notes. Remember to relax after such an attack, as you don't want to feel tense when you play (even if the music is tense).

Dynamic Marks

Here are the most common symbols (from softest to loudest) that indicate how loud to play. You'll find these below the staff. Once introduced, a dynamic mark stays in effect until another symbol appears.

Play Softest ──────────────────────────────────► Play Loudest

ppp	pp	p	mp	mf	f	ff	fff
Pianississimo	Pianissimo	Piano	Mezzo Piano	Mezzo Forte	Forte	Fortissimo	Fortississimo

Crescendo and Decrescendo Marks

A *crescendo* (abbreviated *cresc.*) is a gradual increase in volume while a *descrendo* is a gradual decrease. They are marked by two lines that form an angle. As the angle opens or closes under a passage of notes, the volume of the passage increases or decreases respectively. Even a single note (if it has a longer duration) can be marked with a crescendo or descresendo.

Lesson 2: Navigating the Song

Songs are usually arranged in *sections*. Sections are pieced together like puzzle pieces to create a song's *structure* (form). Since songs tend to repeat sections in creative ways, written music frequently uses special symbols (we'll call them *navigation symbols*) to guide a player from one part of the song to the next. This lesson sheds some light on these terms and their use in songs.

The Verse

A *verse* is a melody over a chord progression. Like in a poem, there can be any number of verses in a song. Each verse may have different lyrics but maintains a consistent rhythm, melody and number of phrases. Traditionally, the word "verse" refers to a set of lyrics, but in modern popular music the word can refer to the combination of chords, lyrics and phrases. Verses make up the bulk of a song.

Some of the most memorable songs are built using only repeating verses and an occasional instrumental break (discussed at the bottom of the next column). "Phrasing the Section" utilized the repeating verse form of Bob Dylan's memorable classic, "All Along the Watchtower."

The Bridge

A *bridge* is a transitional section of a song. Its job is to lead the song from one section to another. Usually, the music is different from the other sections and it may or may not have vocals.

The Chorus

The *chorus* or *refrain* is the part of the song that is inserted between verses. Sometimes, it's preceded by a bridge and it always repeats more than once in a song. Often, the same lyrics are used for each chorus. A song tends to build to a chorus, which has more intensity than the verse.

The Instrumental Break

The *break* is the part of the song where the singing stops and the instruments come to the forefront. It is something like an instrumental chorus and usually repeats a number of times throughout a song. During a break an instrument may play a memorable riff (sometimes called a *hook*) or take a short solo.

The Introduction

An *introduction* or *intro* is a short passage that introduces a song. It can be comprised of riffs, chords or just about any music device, but it is distinct from the verse and usually leads into it smoothly.

The Outro

The term *outro* refers to the ending of a song. Sometimes, it's a return to the music presented in the intro, but it can feature different musical ideas as well.

The Coda

A *coda* is similar to an outro, except that the written music for the coda is separated from the rest of the piece. On a first pass through the music, the coda symbol ⊕ is ignored, but in a repeated section it tells us to jump to the coda music at the end of the piece. The navigation symbols in the right-hand column tell you when to pay attention to the coda symbol.

Navigation Symbols

You already have experience with repeat signs (page 14) and 1st and 2nd endings (page 25). Following are a few more instructions used to flesh out a song's structure.

- *D.C. al Coda (Da Capo al Coda)* tells you to repeat from the beginning of the piece and play to the coda symbol ⊕, at which point you jump to the coda.

- *D.S. al Coda (Dal Segno al Coda)* tells you to repeat from the D.S. symbol 𝄋 and play on until you come to the coda symbol ⊕, at which point you jump to the coda.

- *D.C. al Fine* tells you to repeat from the beginning and play to the word *Fine* (pronounced *fee*-nay), where you end the piece.

- *D.S. al Fine* tells you to repeat from the D.S. symbol 𝄋 and play on until you come to the word *Fine*, where you end.

The Form

The *form* is the structure of a song. It combines different sections and may use repeats and navigation devices. A song's form could be as straight ahead as repeating verses (like Dylan's "All Along the Watchtower" or a traditional storytelling ballad), or it could be a verse–chorus–verse–chorus type form (sometimes called the *A–B–A–B form*). A bridge can be inserted between sections for contrast. For example, verse–chorus–verse–bridge–chorus is a popular song form. Intros, repeats, breaks and codas can spice up the form and make a song more intricate and less predictable.

"Just Like a Song" is a song in the key of D in 6/8 time. In the style of Bob Dylan's "Just Like a Woman," it provides a good example of different sections arranged in an interesting form. You can play it fingerstyle or with an alternating down-up pick motion. But before you do, listen to the CD, while following along with the music. Listen for the section changes, noting the navigation symbols.

Just Like a Song

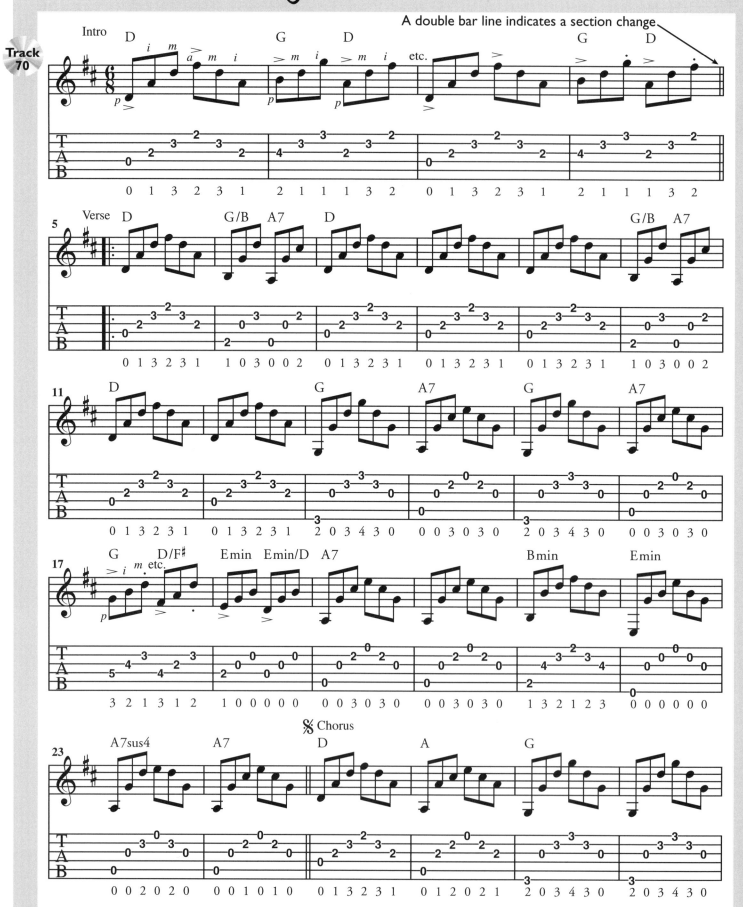

Lesson 3: Tension and Resolution

Creative songwriters take advantage of *tension* produced by unstable musical sounds to make the *resolution* (resolving) to non-tense notes sound even more pleasing to the listener. This technique can help shape phrases and define sections of a piece. The unstable musical sounds mentioned above create *dissonance* (quality of sound that is clashing or unpleasing to the ear), while note combinations that are pleasing to the ear create *consonance*. Of course, good music is in the ears of the listener and what sounds pleasing to one may not sound pleasing to another. But, based on the science of how sound travels in vibrating waves through the air, some note groups physically clash with each other, while other groups of notes vibrate together agreeably.

Degrees of Tension

Different intervals create different amounts of dissonance or consonance. The most consonant (least tense) sounding intervals are the octave (P8), the perfect 4th (P4), the perfect 5th (P5) and the unison (P1). Major 3rds (M3) and minor 3rds (m3) also have a consonant sound to our ears. Other intervals have varying degrees of tension. Play the example below slowly and listen to the sound of each diatonic interval. If you listen very closely, you may notice that some of the intervals create a subtle, quick pulsing sound (this is the clashing sound of dissonance), while others seem to ring evenly (producing the smooth sound of consonance).

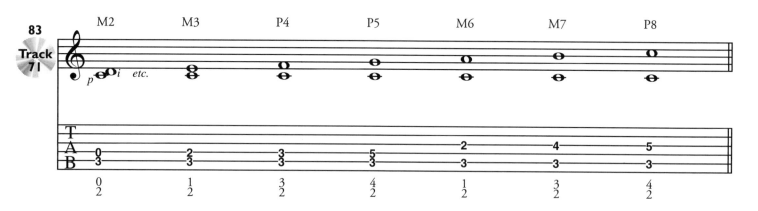

The dominant 7th chord, non-chord tones, altered scale notes, the blues scale and suspended chords are all devices at a songwriter's disposal to create tension and dissonance.

Anticipation

Sometimes guitarists foreshadow an upcoming chord by playing notes from the chord before the actual chord change in the music. This device, called *anticipation*, creates tension that is quickly resolved when the new chord finally arrives. Players like James Taylor and George Harrison have used this technique to create interesting pockets of tension and resolution, giving their songs forward motion and a sense of urgency. Page 99 includes a couple of examples of this.

Try the chord progression below. The unlabeled chord diagram that precedes the C chord is meant to illustrate the fact that your 2nd and 3rd fingers lift off to notes that anticipate the C chord. Similarly, the diagram that precedes the G chord anticipates the open 2nd string of the G chord. The last two measures demonstrate the tension and resolution of suspended chords.

Anticipation Example 1

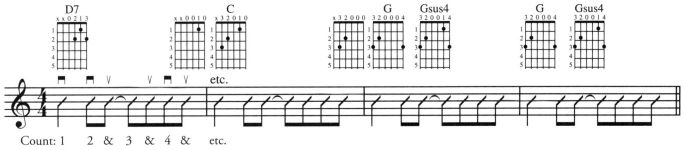

This example is best played fingerstyle. Play it slowly, keeping all notes ringing as long as possible.

Anticipation Example 2

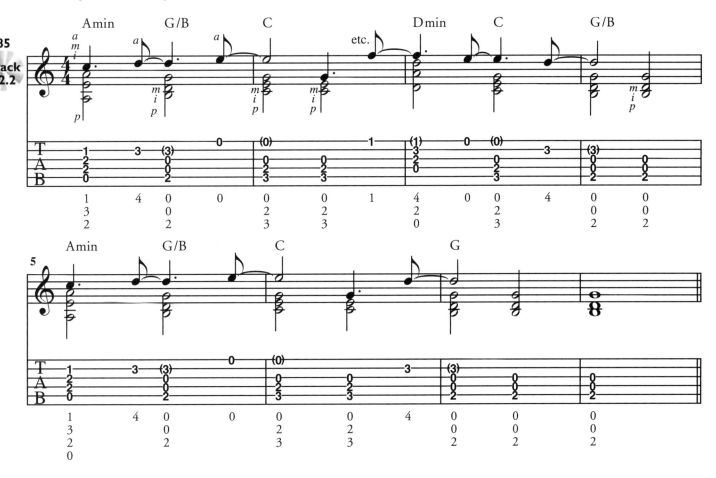

Driving Home "Out" Notes

As we have seen, some note combinations have a naturally consonant quality, but any note—even the most dissonant—will sound right if it is repeated often and played with emphasis. This can be called *driving home the "out" notes.* Songwriters and improvisers often drive home notes or chords that do not naturally fit in the key of the song. This sort of tension doesn't always need to be resolved. In fact, it often becomes the main theme of the song.

Here's a song that combines many tension creating techniques. Its intro, verses and chorus make use of anticipation, suspended chords and seventh chords. Also note how the song builds to the tense-sounding GMaj7 chord. This chord, not normally found in the key of A, eventually becomes the focal point of the song. This song is in the style of James Taylor's "Fire and Rain."

p = Strum chord with downstroke of your thumb.

Departing Tone

Extended Intervals

Sometimes, the distance between two notes is larger than an octave. To name intervals larger than an octave we must understand *scale extensions*. These are scale degree labels given to notes that are over an octave higher than a specified tonic note. Looking at the staff at the top of page 102, you can see that scale degree 8 has the same letter name as scale degree 1. Just as scale degree 2 has the same letter name as scale degree 9, and so on. When we build

intervals using the extended scale degrees 9, 10, 11, 12 and 13, these intervals have the same qualities as the smaller intervals of the same letter names. So, a 9th has the same quality as a 2nd, a 10th has the same quality as a 3rd, an 11th has the same quality as a 4th, and so on.

C Scale with Extended Intervals

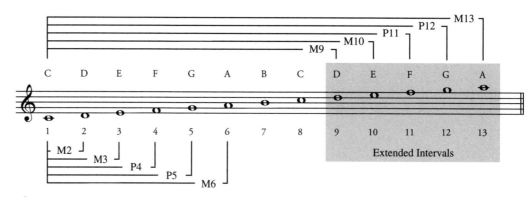

Dominant 9th and Dominant 13th Chords

In Chapter 4 (page 33), you learned that chords are built in 3rds. Triads use scale degrees 1–3–5. Seventh chords add a 3rd above that using the degrees 1–3–5–7. If we carry this concept of *stacking 3rds* into the extended scale, we can add the scale extensions 9–11–13. These are sometimes called *upper extensions*. In theory, a big, fat, colorful chord could use degrees 1–3–5–7–9–11–13 all at once. In practice (on the six-string guitar anyway), we usually add one scale extension at a time to a dominant 7th chord, sometimes losing a note of the triad in the process. You will frequently run across chord symbols such as C9, C11 or C13. These are dominant 7th chords with an added upper extension. (The number written in the chord symbol is the added upper extension). Players like Eric Clapton, Paul Simon and Joni Mitchell often use dominant 9ths, dominant 11ths and dominant 13ths to create a colorful sound that pulls their songs into the realm of jazz.

3rds across the Extended Scale

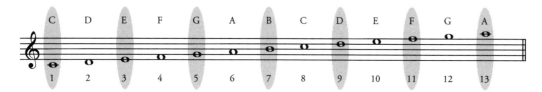

To the right are two typical movable dominant 9th and dominant 13th chord voicings, and below is a verse, in the style of Eric Clapton's "Layla," that uses them.

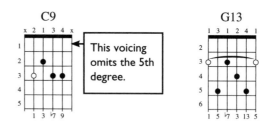

This voicing omits the 5th degree.

Dominant and Intense

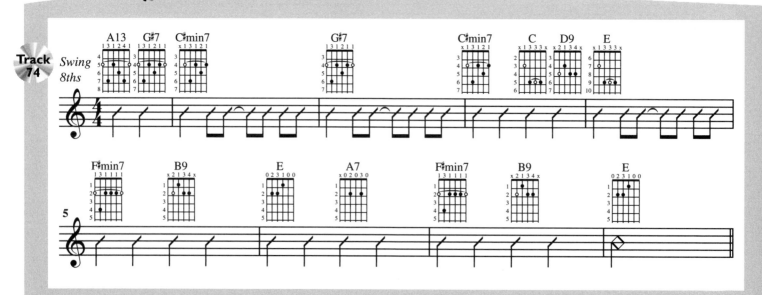

Track 74 · Swing 8ths

This folk-rock song, based on Paul Simon's "Loves Me Like a Rock," utilizes dominant 9th and 13th chords in its chorus. Note that diagrams for all the chords are presented in order of appearance above the written music. Pay special attention to these as new chords are introduced in this song.

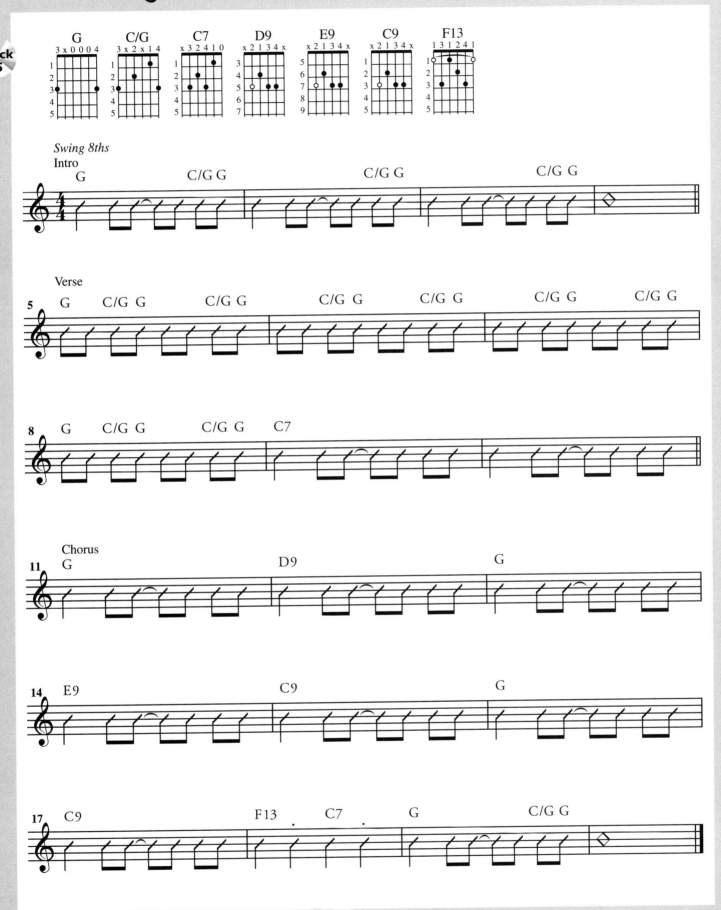

Using Consonant Intervals

Now, let's balance our musical vocabulary by exploring the consonant sounds of 3rds, 6ths and 10ths. These three intervals (considered pleasing since the days that the instrument of choice for singer-songwriters was the lute) are widely used in modern music. Since they are comfortable to move around on the guitar, guitarists like Jim Croce, George Harrison and Paul Simon have used them extensively in their songs. Let's learn them in the key of G, but remember that the fingerings presented are movable and can be shifted to any key.

G Major Scale Harmonized in 6ths

Before harmonizing the scale, let's start by playing the 1st string alone, with only the 1st finger. Notice this is a G Major scale. Now, go back and play both strings, following the fingerings below the TAB. If you play this with a pick, you must muffle the 2nd string with the pad of your 2nd or 3rd finger. If you play it fingerstyle, then you can use your thumb (p) on the 3rd string and your index (i) finger on the 1st string. Notice that this entire harmonized scale is played using only two different fingering shapes.

1st and 3rd Strings

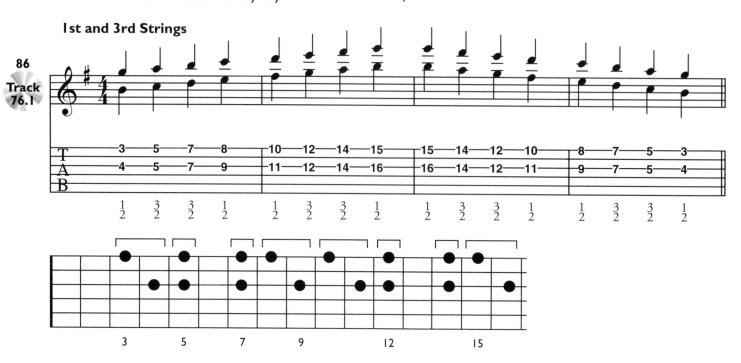

This next example is based on the G Major scale. It is harmonized in 6ths on the 2nd and 4th strings. Again, mute the inner string with the pad of your 2nd or 3rd finger as you strum across three strings—or use the p and i fingers

to play this fingerstyle. Note that the fretboard diagram and the example in standard music notation do not start on the same interval. This is because the diagram shows the intervals from lowest to highest on the fretboard.

2nd and 4th Strings

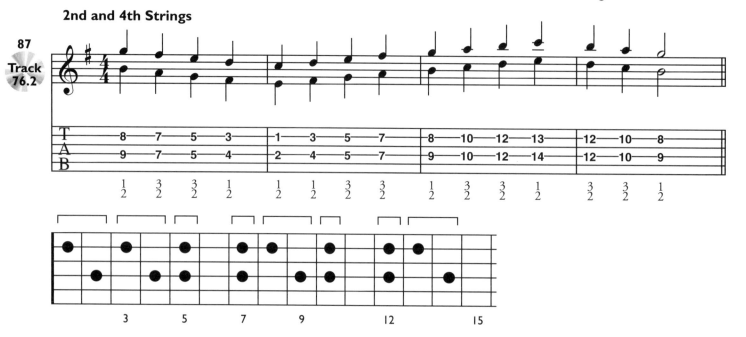

G Major Scale Harmonized in 3rds

Below are two fingerings that take you across the scale in 3rds, first on the 1st and 2nd strings, then on the 2nd and 3rd strings. The 3rds are usually on adjacent strings so they are easy to play with the pick. As with 6ths, it is possible to play 3rds fingerstyle with the *p* and *i* fingers.

1st and 2nd Strings

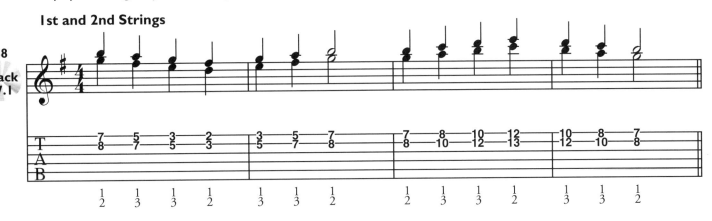

2nd and 3rd Strings

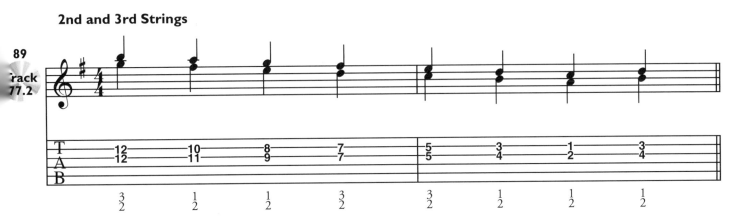

G Major Scale Harmonized in 10ths

Perhaps the fullest sounding consonant interval is the 10th. Remember, the notes of this interval are over an octave apart so it is not conducive to playing with the pick unless you use the hybrid picking technique introduced on page 83. Use your *p* and *i* fingers to play this scale harmonized in 10ths.

G Major Scale in 10ths

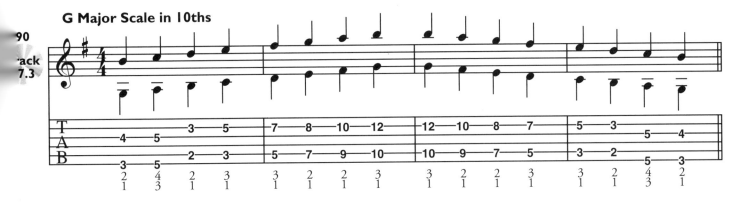

"Short and Sweet" is in the style of Jim Croce and George Harrison. The intro uses moving 6ths played against a pedal tone on the open D string. In the verse, there are fills off the D7 chord at the end of each chord sequence. They use 10ths, 6ths and 3rds. Take advantage of open strings to help you perform big position shifts. For example, to get to the fill in measure 12 in time, move your hand to the 6th position as you play the last two open notes of the previous measure.

Short and Sweet

Chapter 11: Advanced Techniques

This chapter discusses alternate ways to pull sound from the acoustic guitar. Songwriters and improvisers use the techniques discussed here to vary the texture of their music. The use of *alternate tunings,* the *bottleneck slide, harmonics* and *tapping* can expand the range and color of the guitar. We'll explore these tunings and techniques and discuss how innovative guitarists like Joni Mitchell, Michael Hedges, Leo Kottke, Ani DiFranco and Jimmy Page have used them in their music.

Lesson 1: Alternate Tunings

In search of new ways to build tension and resolution into their songs, guitarist-songwriters often tune some or all of their strings to different pitches. The tuning we've used up to this point (E–A–D–G–B–E) is called *standard tuning.* Any tuning that differs from standard tuning is an *alternate tuning.* For as long as the acoustic guitar has existed, guitarists have experimented with alternate tunings. The original Delta blues players often tuned their open strings to major or minor chords (these are *open tunings*). This allowed them to easily locate the I, IV and V chords and to resolve to the I chord (which would be the open strings) at any moment. Exploring creative new alternate tunings as well as traditional open tunings, the guitarist-songwriter Joni Mitchell used tunings to achieve drone notes (emulating the Appalachian mountain dulcimer) and to facilitate fingerings for the upper extensions (9th, 11th and 13th). Many acoustic guitarists like Tracy Chapman, Neil Young and David Crosby employ alternate tunings to accomplish new textures for their songs. As they all prove, the possibilities for new applications of open tunings are endless.

This lesson focuses on a few traditional open tunings used extensively by songsters like Robert Johnson, Joni Mitchell and John Prine. Lesson 4 (page 122) introduces the slightly more radical alternate tuning, Dsus4 (also known as DADGAD).

*To many, the music of **Robert Johnson** is the epitome of the blues. In 1930, partly inspired by bluesman Son House, Johnson left the world of sharecropping to become a full-time musician. In his short career, he recorded 29 songs. These intense recordings represent some of the most influential blues music ever produced.*

COURTESY OF DELTA HAZE CORPORATION

Open G Tuning

Open G tuning is a popular open tuning. It's great to start with because the adjacent 2nd, 3rd and 4th strings remain tuned to their standard pitches. Because of this, you can use these strings for standard chord fingerings while using the altered strings for drone tones or to produce new textures. The altered strings are tuned down to the nearest note of the G triad (G–B–D). In open G tuning your 6th, 5th and 1st strings are tuned down a whole step as indicated in the staff and TAB to the right. In this book, the new pitches for open strings in alternate tunings are indicated at the beginning of each TAB staff.

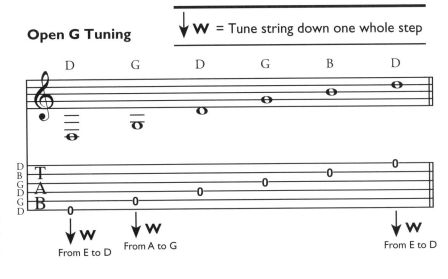

There are a number of ways to get into this open tuning. You can use an electronic tuner (especially a chromatic tuner, which tunes any pitch) to assist you in the effort. If you liked the relative tuning approach (page 9), you can use the fretboard diagram to the right (after lowering your 6th string a whole step to D) to tune one string to the next. Note that you can tune your 6th string down to D by matching the pitch (but an octave below) of the open D (4th) string.

Relative Tuning Diagram for Open G Tuning

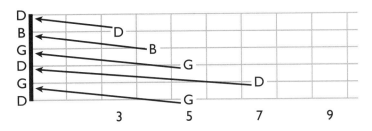

Before we learn a song using this tuning, let's try recognizing some chord shapes on the 2nd, 3rd and 4th strings. This approach may help you get started using this tuning to create your own songs. Below are chord diagrams (top row) with fingering dots in gray or solid black. Form the solid dots on the 2nd, 3rd and 4th strings and examine how they relate to the full fingerings of standard tuning

(the solid and gray dots combined). These fingerings are used in the short example that follows against drone notes of the open G tuning. Don't let the new chord symbols throw you off; new chords are created by the tensions introduced with drone strings.

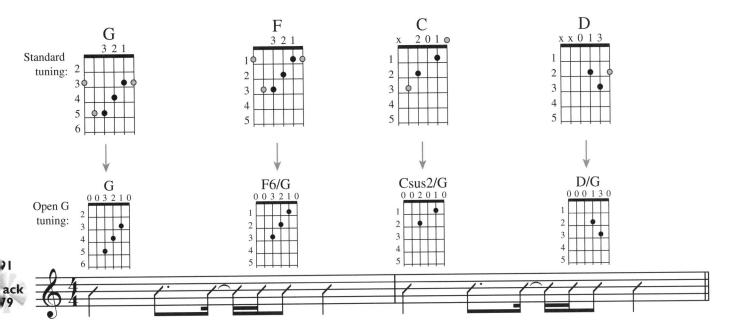

Another important aspect of open G tuning is the location of the I, IV and V chords. Since the open strings are tuned to a G chord, they form the I chord of the key. You can easily form the IV chord just by barring across all six strings at the 5th fret. Similarly, you get the V chord by barring the 7th fret. These same locations for the primary chords are found in all open tunings. They have been used extensively by blues players to play the 12-bar blues progression as well as by modern acoustic guitarists seeking to incorporate some bluesy sounds into their music.

Following is an example of the 12-bar blues progression in open G tuning. It has a blues style intro and ending that take full advantage of the open strings. Also, watch out for the double-string hammer-ons; make sure your left-hand fingers clear the open strings when hammering-on so that the open strings keep ringing.

Open G Blues

"That's the Way of the Circle Song" is played in open G tuning. It uses many of the concepts we've just talked about. The song's intro is in the style of early Joni Mitchell and is best played fingerstyle. The constant open 3rd string in the intro displays how open strings can ring as dissonances and then resolve over a series of chords. As the intro ends with a long ringing whole note, you have time to pick up your pick and get ready to strum the verse. Many guitarists, like Jimmy Page, add variety to their music by switching between pick style and fingerstyle, even within a single song. The verse and bridge in this song are in the style of Page's strumming in Led Zeppelin's "That's the Way." Eventually, the song leads to a chorus that takes advantage of the I–IV–V positions used by many blues players, as well as rock bands like the Rolling Stones and the Black Crowes. Finally, the tune comes full circle as the song ends with an outro that's a subtle variation on the fingerpicking intro.

Try revisiting pages 94–95, which discuss typical sections of songs. Then, try your hand at song construction by rearranging the sections of this tune into a form other than the one written here.

That's the Way of the Circle Song

Open D Tuning

Open D tuning is another popular alternate tuning. Only the 4th (D) and 5th (A) strings keep their original pitch, while the rest of the strings must be tuned down.

↓ **H** = Tune string down one half step

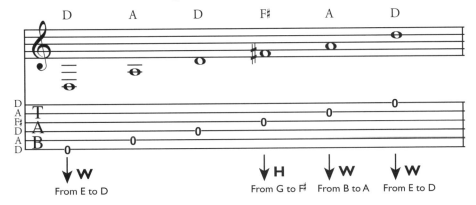

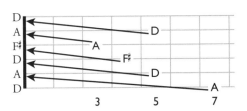

Because only two strings keep their original pitches, it is not as easy to relate open D to standard forms as it is with open G, but some of the ideas and shapes that work well in open G also work in open D. For instance, the shape that we label on page 109 as Csus2/G works well in this tuning, but you must shift your fingers to the next set of lower strings. Also, the positions of the primary chords are the same as in open G tuning: open (I chord), 5th (IV chord) and 7th (V chord). Following is a blues turnaround that demonstrates the similarities between open D and open G. This one is possible to play with your pick. Notice how easy it is to insert a I chord between the other chords.

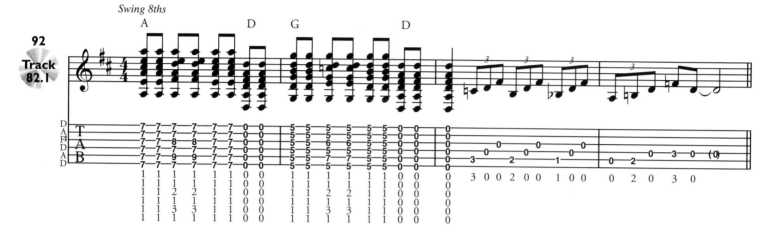

"Turn on Your Big Yellow Radio" is in the style of songs Joni Mitchell wrote in open tunings. This song displays similarities between open G and open D. It also demonstrates how easy it is to create big, colorful chords in open tunings—with simple fingerings—against a lot of open notes. Remember, the × symbols represent mute strokes.

Turn on Your Big Yellow Radio

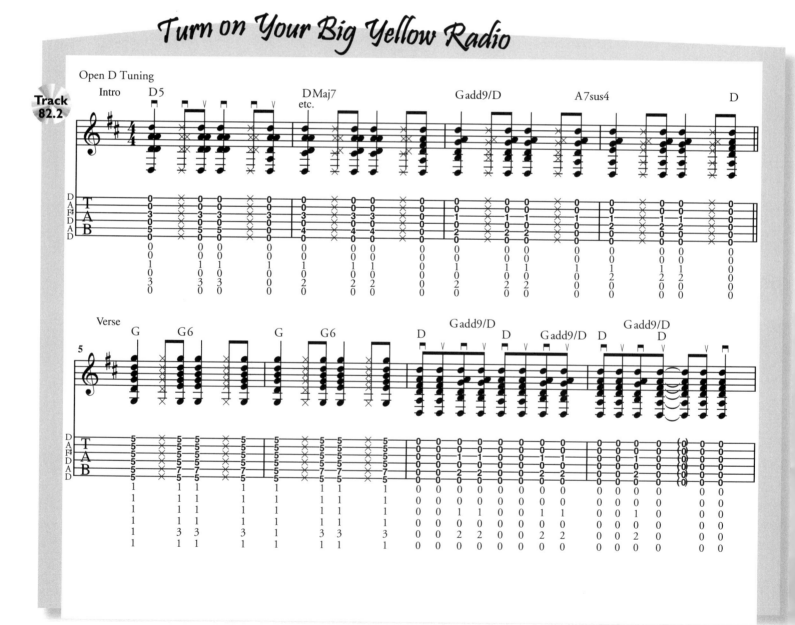

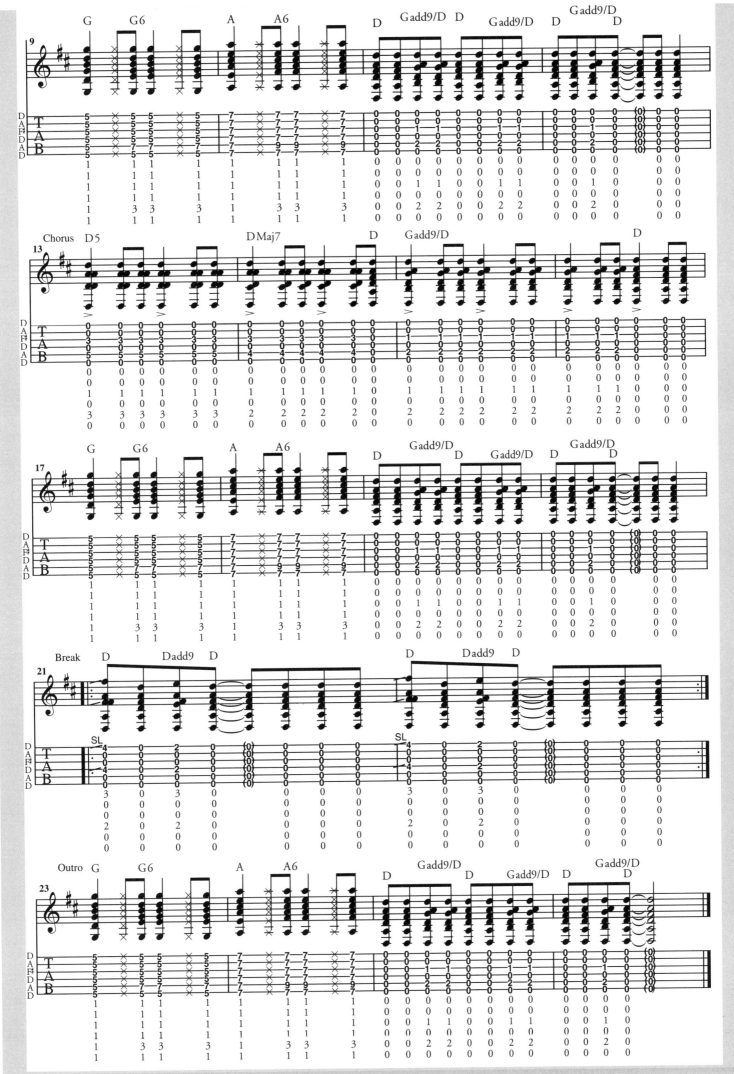

Some More Common Alternate Tunings

Each time that you tune your strings differently, doors open to new areas of texture. If you like endless possibilities, you may want to continue experimenting with alternate tunings. Following are some more of the most common open tunings. Both *open A tuning* and *open E tuning* involve *tightening* strings to reach higher pitches. Do this carefully, as tight strings (especially old ones) can break. Also, if you wish to use these tunings often, you may want to visit a *guitar luthier* (someone who makes and repairs guitars) or your local guitar shop for suggestions on the best strings for your needs.

Open A Tuning

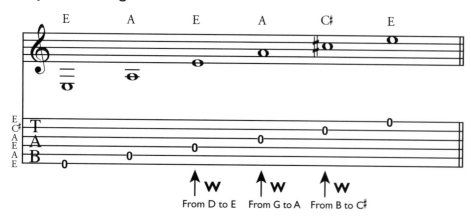
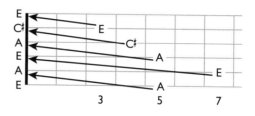

Open E Tuning

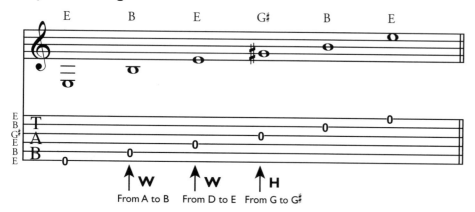
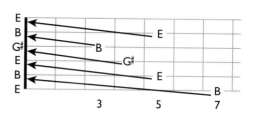

Alternate Tunings and the Capo

Remember, clamping on a capo at different frets allows you to change keys and keep the same open fingerings. This is especially effective with open tunings. Guitarists use the capo to shift fingerings to keys that work better for a singer's vocal range. Below is a chart that will help you determine which fret to place a capo on so you can play in different keys while in open G, open D, open A or open E tuning.

Fret	0	1	2	3	4	5	6	7	8	9	10
Key in open G	G	A♭	A	B♭	B	C	D♭	D	E♭	E	F
Key in open D	D	E♭	E	F	G♭	G	A♭	A	B♭	B	C
Key in open A	A	B♭	B	C	D♭	D	E♭	E	F	G♭	G
Key in open E	E	F	G♭	G	A♭	A	B♭	B	C	D♭	D

Lesson 2: The Bottleneck Slide

Many guitarists use a *slide* on a left-hand finger to produce a fluid, or smooth, transition between notes or chords. Slides come in many varieties (glass, metal, porcelain; thick, thin, long, short, etc.) and produce a vocal-like quality as they "slide" across the guitar strings. The slide technique, thought to originate in Hawaii, quickly found a home in blues and country music. Blues players would use bottlenecks, knives and even pipes to get the slide effect. Since its conception, countless guitarists have used the slide in many genres to vary the color of the guitar.

Using the Slide

Most guitarists wear the slide on their pinky or 3rd finger. This leaves the other fingers free to fret notes. Also, fingers behind the slide (closer to the nut) are placed across the strings to stop unwanted ringing. Slide players use either the pick or right-hand fingers to attack notes. (We'll use fingers for our examples.) In either case, they use free fingers to damp upper strings that are adjacent to attacked strings and the palm to damp lower strings. The slide must be placed directly over the fret wire to play notes with proper *intonation*, or notes that are in tune. Once you have a slide, try Example 93 using the following steps as guidelines. Notice that slides (SL) achieved with or without a slide on a left-hand finger are notated the same way.

Correct slide placement.

1. Place the slide on either your pinky or 3rd finger (whichever is more comfortable to you).

2. Line the slide up to the 5th fret and place all your fingers across all six strings. If the slide is on your 3rd finger, lift your pinky slightly off the strings. The fingers behind the slide take care of the left-hand damping.

3. Now, for the right-hand damping, rest the palm of your right hand on the 6th, 5th and 4th strings. Also, rest your *m* finger on the 2nd string. (This is the adjacent string to the attacked string.)

4. For your first note, attack the 3rd string with your index *(i)* finger and then move your entire left hand up two frets. Your slide should stop directly above the 7th fret.

5. Let's reverse the procedure to get our second note. With your slide still at the 7th fret, attack the 3rd string and bring the slide back to the 5th fret. Remember to keep your left-hand fingers down behind the slide and to damp the 2nd string with your free *m* finger.

6. To finish the riff, your right hand needs to cross strings so move your *m* finger and palm one string lower. (Now your *m* finger is damping the 3rd string, while your palm is damping the 5th and 6th strings.) Attack the 4th string with your index *(i)* finger and slide your whole hand up, stopping the slide directly above the 7th fret.

93

Track 83.1

Slide Example

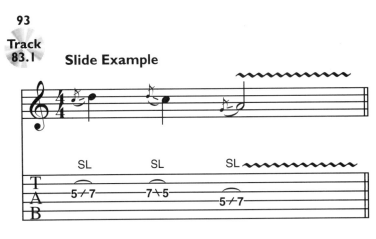

Slide players often rock the slide back and forth horizontally on longer notes. This vibrato effect mimics the similar effect used by vocalists. The key to good vibrato is keeping the fret at the exact center of the rocking motion. This produces a full, round vibrato that sounds in tune.

Using the Slide in Open Tuning

The slide can be used in standard tuning to play riffs and outline the scale forms that you have learned. It also can be used with open tunings. A staple of the Delta blues sound, slide use has been incorporated by many modern players. The fingerstyle virtuoso Leo Kottke incorporated the slide into his open-tuned instrumentals. Based on traditional blues progressions and riffs, his slide work sometimes incorporated drums and bass to produce an aggressive rock-like feel. Similarly, to support vocals, Jimmy Page incorporated open slide work into some Led Zeppelin tunes.

Open tunings make it easy to move chords around with the slide. Although they focus on the open, 5th and 7th frets (the positions for the I, IV and V chords), players like Kottke and Page expanded blues slide playing by incorporating more positions and chords. "Stompin' Machine" is in open G tuning. It makes use of a fingerstyle pattern like those used by Kottke and a single-string slide riff similar to some blues slide licks borrowed by Page. As you fingerpick the chords in this piece, make sure your slide is lined up directly above the frets. Don't hesitate to add a little vibrato (centered on the fret) here and there. Note that all closed notes are produced by the slide.

Stompin' Machine

Lesson 3: Harmonics

The sound of a vibrating string is actually made up of a series of sounds that combine to produce the overall tone of the string. The main pitch that we hear is called the *fundamental*. Above it there is a set of pitches called the *overtone series*, which is different for each type of instrument. We can recognize the sound of a guitar versus that of a flute (even when they play the same note) due to their different set of overtones.

With the right touch, guitarists are able to bypass the fundamental pitch of a string and bring out the sound of the string's overtones. We call these unique sounds *harmonics*. Harmonics are pure, chime-like tones that are usually high pitched and distinct from open or fretted notes. We'll learn two types of harmonics: natural and artificial.

Natural Harmonics

When you attack an open string you hear mostly the fundamental pitch. However, there are three primary locations on a string where it is possible to single out specific harmonics called *natural harmonics* because they are easy to produce on an open string. Their locations are directly above the 12th fret, 7th fret and 5th fret. Notice that these spots divide the strings into simple fractions. The 12th fret divides the string in half, the 7th fret in thirds and the 5th in quarters.

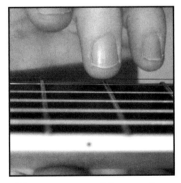

Playing a natural harmonic.

To play a natural harmonic, just barely touch a string directly above one of the frets mentioned above, right above the fret wire. Give the string a firm pick and quickly move your finger away from the string. When you get the timing right, you'll hear a long-lasting, bell-like tone. Try this at the 12th fret first as it produces the strongest natural harmonic.

Natural Harmonics on a Single String

In the example below, you will see the open-E fundamental and the natural harmonics on the 6th string. On the staff, diamonds ◇ are used as noteheads to indicate harmonics. The actual sounding pitch is written on the staff unless accompanied by the symbol 8va, which means that the actual pitch is one octave higher than written. Expect the harmonic with this symbol to sound one octave higher than the staff location. In TAB, a diamond placed above a fret number tells you to produce a harmonic at that fret. Try this example on some other strings as well.

◇ = Harmonic

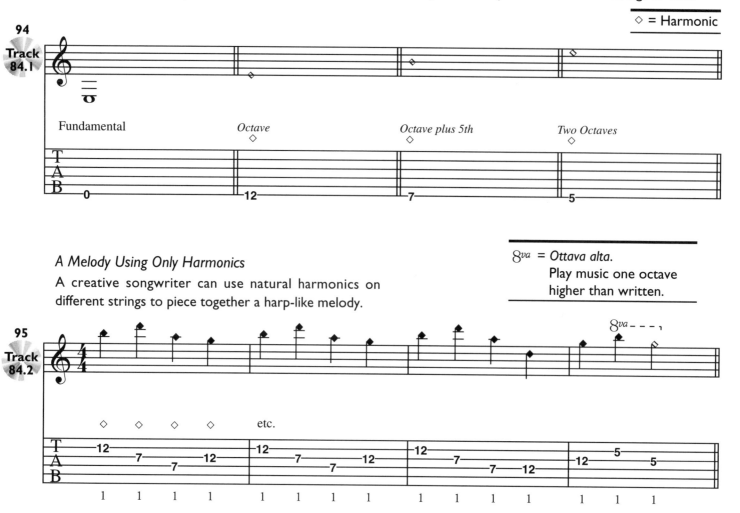

A Melody Using Only Harmonics

A creative songwriter can use natural harmonics on different strings to piece together a harp-like melody.

8va = Ottava alta.
Play music one octave higher than written.

Natural Harmonics on Multiple Strings

It is possible to sound harmonics on multiple strings at once. To do this, you must very lightly and evenly place a finger across the strings. The 1st, 2nd or 3rd fingers work best. Be careful not to bend your joints, as this will affect even placement. Attack the strings and quickly pull your finger away just as you did on the single strings. You must pull away as evenly as you placed your finger. Try this riff that mixes single and multiple string harmonics.

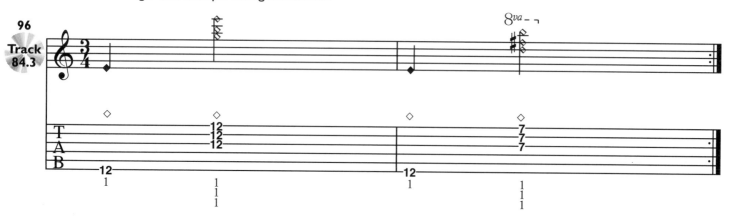

Artificial Harmonics

You can also use *any* fretted note as a fundamental pitch for a set of harmonics. These are called *artificial harmonics (A.H.)* because we must change a string's length to get them. It takes two hands to coordinate artificial harmonics. Your left hand changes a string's length by placing a finger behind a fret while the index finger of your right hand barely touches the string exactly 5, 7 or 12 frets higher than the fretted note, directly above the fret wire (see Photo 1). To sound the harmonic, you attack the string with your right-hand thumb in a downward motion (see Photo 2). Some players prefer to use their ring *(a)* finger in an upward motion instead.

It will take a while to get your right hand comfortable performing artificial harmonics, but once it does you'll find creative ways to use artificial harmonics. Below is Form 1 of the D Major Pentatonic scale played with artificial harmonics 12 frets above the fret numbers in the TAB. Note that the frets at which your right-hand finger touches the string is indicated above the standard music notation with Roman numerals.

Photo 1

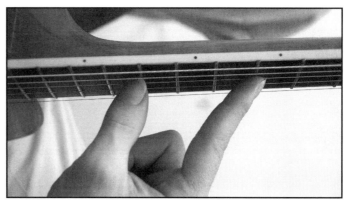

Photo 2

$\underset{\diamond}{A.H.}$ = Artificial harmonic

Pentatonic Run with Artificial Harmonics

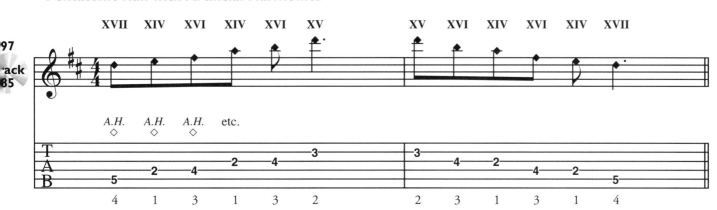

Lesson 4: Tapping and Slapping

When a right-hand hammer-on is used (instead of a pick attack) to set off the vibration of a string, the motion is called a *tap* (T). Usually, taps are combined with regular hammer-ons and pull-offs to connect a musical phrase.

This technique is called *tapping*. The acoustic guitarist and composer Michael Hedges is remembered for extending acoustic tapping techniques to simultaneous strings. He also incorporated two hands into his tapping. We'll discuss the left-hand tapping first.

Dsus4 Tuning (DADGAD)

Before we explore the tapping technique, let's get into an alternate tuning that works well for the techniques in this lesson. This tuning is not based on a triad, instead the strings are tuned to the unresolved sound of a Dsus4 chord. The 6th, 2nd and 1st strings are tuned down one

whole step to D, A and D, respectively, while the 5th, 4th and 3rd stay in standard pitch. Sometimes the tuning is referred to by its string pitches, *DADGAD*. Besides Hedges, many other guitarists have used this tuning including Joni Mitchell, Ani DiFranco and Jimmy Page.

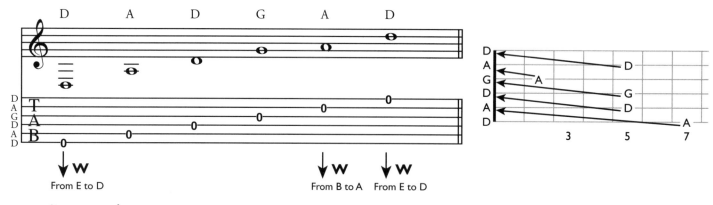

Left-Hand Tapping

We'll focus on expanding our left-hand hammer-ons and pull-offs into tapping. When combining hammer-ons and pull-offs with tapping, hammer the strings with your fingertips very close to the fret wires, then pull your fingers off the strings with a slight plucking motion. This will keep

the sound strong and active. The two exercises below will help you build dexterity. Play them slowly at first. Speed them up only as your taps, hammers and pulls-offs become louder and more even-sounding.

Single-String Tapping Exercise

T = Tap

98 Track 86.1

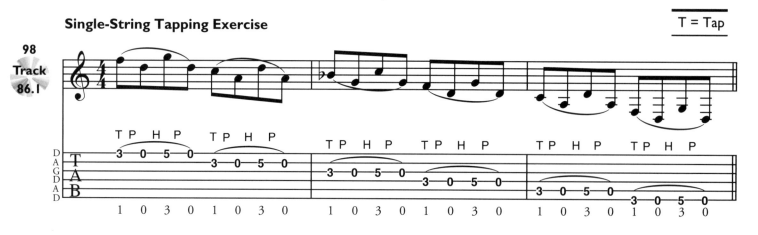

Multiple-String Tapping Exercise

99 Track 86.2

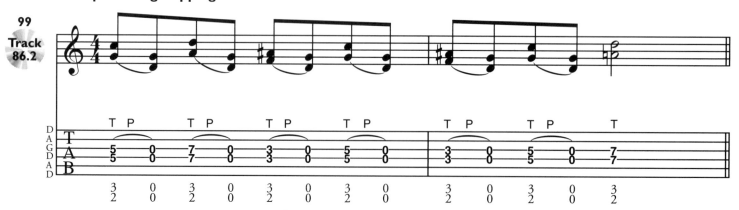

Slap Harmonics

Another technique used by acoustic guitarists like Michael Hedges and Ani DiFranco is the *slap harmonic (S.H.)*. It's a sharp, percussive harmonic chord made by reaching over the top of the neck with the right hand (see Photo 1) and *slapping* the strings with the middle or index finger, whichever is more comfortable for you (see Photo 2). This technique works best at the locations of the natural harmonics (the 12th, 7th and 5th frets) and it is usually used in open tunings.

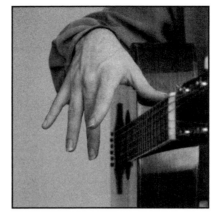

Photo 1

Make sure that you are still tuned to DADGAD and try a slap harmonic on the 12th fret:

1. Line up the middle or index finger of your right hand directly over the 12th fret. It must be aligned perfectly with the fret wire.

2. Now, keeping parallel to the fret, lift your finger away from the strings.

3. Finally, strike directly above the 12th fret with a sharp snap of the wrist, pulling away as soon as you make contact with the strings. You don't need to strike hard to make the harmonics sound and only slightly harder to produce the percussive sound of the strings snapping against the fret.

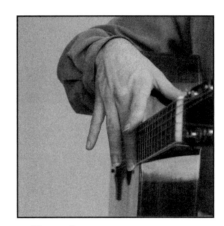

Photo 2

Following the steps above will produce a chord that has a very different sound than fretted chords or chords produced by the other types of harmonics. Since it takes only your right hand to perform slap harmonics, this technique is useful when you want to create a two-part texture. If your right hand slaps harmonics on the lower strings, your left hand is free to tap notes. Try this example (still in Dsus4 tuning) of slapped chords supporting a tapped melody.

S.H. = Slap harmonic
◇

Two-Part Slapping and Tapping Example

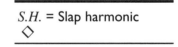

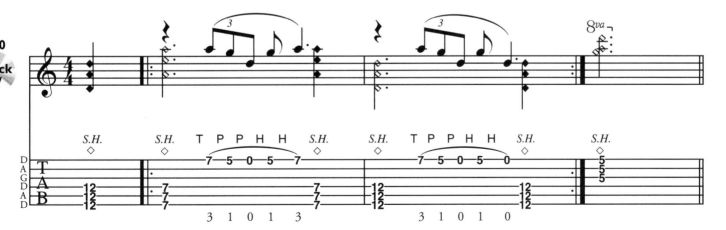

Here's a piece that makes use of slap, natural and artificial harmonics as well as the advanced technique of tapping. To play it, your strings should be tuned to DADGAD. Don't hesitate to let notes ring for longer than their written value. As you allow bass notes to sustain under melodies that use harmonics you will hear a full two-part sound.

Moonbeam Bridge

Lesson 5: World Influences

As you get comfortable with the different styles and techniques presented in this book, you may find yourself combining them in your own songs and improvisations. To further this development and discover new creative rhythms and textures, keep your ears open to musical influences from around the world.* As volumes could be written on world music, this chapter only briefly describes a few main points about some genres that have greatly influenced innovative acoustic guitar songwriters and composers.

Afro-Cuban and Latin Influence

Many forms of Latin music make use of a rhythmic pattern called the *clave*. Developed in Cuba with African roots, it found its way into many Latin styles as well as the Brazilian *bossa nova*. The basic clave is accented in a 3-2 feel, or reversed to create a 2-3 feel.

3-2 Clave Rhythm

101
Track 89.1

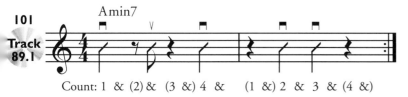

Count: 1 & (2) & (3 &) 4 & (1 &) 2 & 3 & (4 &)

102
Track 89.2

Count: (1 &) 2 & 3 & (4 &) 1 & (2) & (3 &) 4 &

The clave rhythm is often played on percussion instruments, especially by two wooden sticks (called *claves*) that are hit together. When it is interpreted on the guitar, the guitarist usually plays the clave rhythm on the upper strings and accompanies it with a bass line on beats 1 and 3. As with the bossa nova style, the clave rhythm is often loosely interpreted and used as a base on which the guitarist improvises. A lot of music has incorporated this Latin feel, such as João Gilberto's playing in the 1960s and even Jack Johnson's most recent work.

Clave Guitar Rhythm

03
ack
9.3

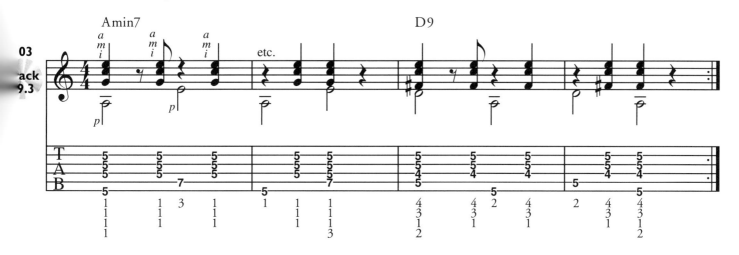

* Check out Alfred/National Guitar Workshop's *Guitar Atlas Series: Guitar Music from Around the Globe*. This series presents music from around the world (Africa, Middle East, Brazil, India, etc.) adapted primarily for the acoustic guitar.

La Pompe and the Gypsy Swing Feel

In the 1930s, the legendary gypsy guitarist Django Reinhardt pioneered a style of acoustic guitar playing that combined elements of American swing with the tense colorings of gypsy music. Coined *gypsy jazz*, the style uses a distinct, percussive rhythm guitar technique called *la pompe*. It consists of chords strummed in continuous quarter notes, which are played staccato on beats 2 and 4. The point of release on the staccato beats gives the rhythm a swing eighths feel, even though eighth notes are not played. One of the most popular forms in this genre is referred to as *rhythm changes* (after George Gershwin's "I Got Rhythm"). The form consists of four 8-measure sections (the first eight measures are repeated and make up the Section 2). Sections 1, 2 and 4 are essentially the same, while the 3rd (the bridge) differs from the rest. Listen to the CD to hear how the staccato releases on beats 2 and 4 maintain the swing feel.

La Pompe over Rhythm Changes

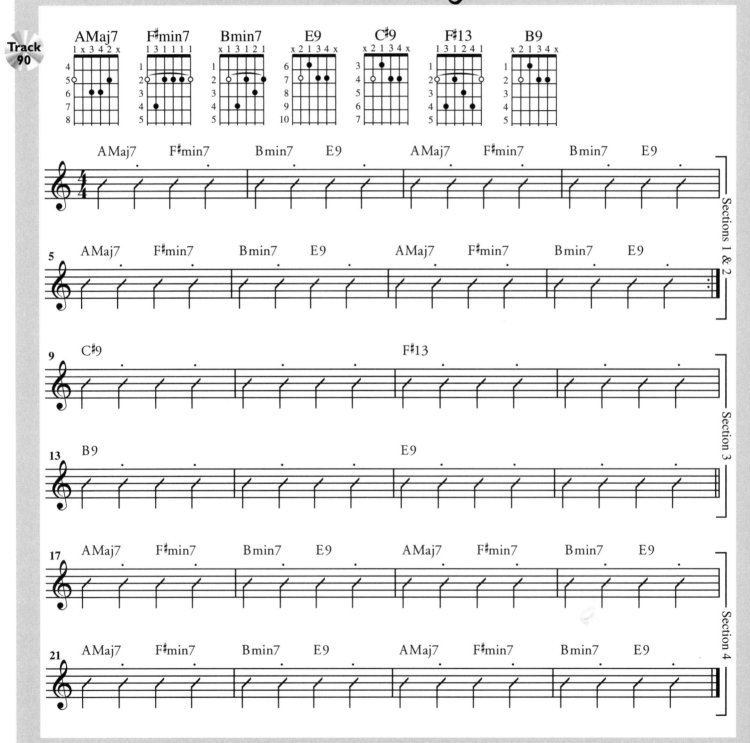

126 The Total Acoustic Guitarist

Celtic Influence

In the 1960s, groups like the Chieftains and Fairport Convention sometimes incorporated rhythm guitar playing to accompany traditional Irish and Celtic melodies (which are thought to have been played originally without accompaniment). This rhythmic style now associated with Celtic guitar playing, incorporates open tunings, drone strings and heavy syncopation in $\frac{6}{8}$ time. To get a feel for this sort of strumming try the example below. Follow the pick motion and accents carefully, as the upstroke on the second accented beat is an important part of this feel.

Accenting the Celtic Strum

04

ack
1.1

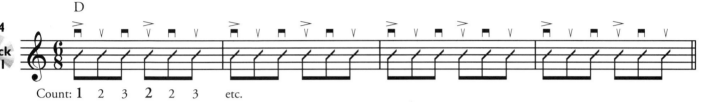

Tune your 6th string down one whole step to D for this next example. This is called *drop D tuning*. The example emulates the signature drone tone of the bagpipes. Follow the pick motion closely at measure 7 and 8, as it creates a syncopated feel that can be tricky to play.

Celtic Style Syncopation

95

ack
.2

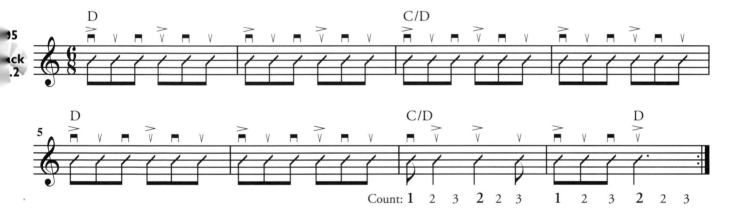

Final Thoughts

Congratulations, you've gotten down the basics of acoustic guitar playing, explored many advanced techniques and learned about song structure. Hopefully, you're having a great time incorporating many new concepts into your playing. Now, continue to use this knowledge in context. Play with others any chance you get; construct new tunes and listen, listen, listen. As you listen to CDs, try to recognize the concepts and techniques you've explored between these covers. After some time away from this book, you may wish to revisit some chapters and explore the lessons with your new ears and new chops. Keep learning in any way you can. A good teacher can help you considerably as can other books and DVDs. Above all, remember to enjoy music and stay open to new musical influences, as these can enrich your playing and creative potential.

If you have any questions about the material in this book, you can write to franknatterjr@faceartsstudio.com.

If you love this book,
you'll love our schools!

Online...

WL
WORKSHOPLIVE

The next generation of music
education from the founders of the
National Guitar Workshop

Take a FREE online
lesson today.
workshoplive.com

...or Near You!

N·G·W
National Guitar
Workshop

LOCATIONS: Connecticut, Florida
Seattle, Nashville, Los Angeles,
Texas, San Francisco, Virginia

1-800-234-6479
guitarworkshop.com